DISCOVERING CAREERS FOR YOUR FUTURE

food

Ferguson
An imprint of ☑® Facts On File

Discovering Careers for Your Future: Food

Copyright © 2005 by Facts On File, Inc.

Ferguson
An imprint of Facts On File, Inc.
132 West 31st Street
New York NY 10001

Discovering careers for your future. Food.
    p. cm.
Includes index.
    ISBN 0-8160-5848-2 (hc : alk. paper)
    1. Food service—Vocational guidance. I. Title: Food. II. J.G. Ferguson Publishing Company.
    TX911.2.D575 2005
    647.95'023—dc22   2005003299

Ferguson books are available at special discounts when purchased in bulk quantities for businesses, associations, institutions, or sales promotions. Please call our Special Sales Department in New York at (212) 967-8800 or (800) 322-8755.

You can find Ferguson on the World Wide Web at http://www.fergpubco.com

Text design by Mary Susan Ryan-Flynn

Printed in the United States of America

EB FOF 10 9 8 7 6 5 4 3 2 1

This book is printed on acid-free paper.

Contents

Introduction

You may not have decided yet what you want to be in the future. And you don't have to decide right away. You do know that right now you are interested in careers in the food industry. Do any of the following statements describe you? If so, you may want to begin thinking about what a career in the food industry might mean for you.

___I enjoy reading about food and food history.
___I enjoy cooking for my friends and family.
___I like to write stories.
___I like to teach others.
___I like to discover new restaurants or kinds of food and tell my friends about them.
___I enjoy gardening.
___I am responsible for feeding and caring for our family pet.
___I enjoy coming up with my own recipes.
___I belong to a 4-H Club or Future Farmers of America.
___My parents are farmers and I would like to continue the family business.
___I enjoy conducting experiments.
___I collect specimens to view under my microscope.
___I like to fish.
___I enjoy learning about and trying foods from other cultures.
___I enjoy learning about healthy and unhealthy foods.
___I like to give directions to other people.

Discovering Careers for Your Future: Food is a book about careers in the food industry, from bakers to farmers to supermarket managers. Careers in this field can be found on farms, in factories, in publishing companies, in classrooms, in business offices, in restaurants, on ships, in wineries and breweries, in supermarkets, and in countless other settings.

This book describes many possibilities for a future in the food industry. Read through it and see how the different careers are connected. For example, if you are interested in working outdoors, you should read the chapters on farmers, fishers, and grain merchants. If you are interested in cooking, you will want to read the chapters about cooking instructors and cooks and chefs. If you are interested in writing about food, read about cookbook and recipe writers, food writers and editors, and other careers. If you are interested in the manufacturing and production aspects of this field, you will want to read about beverage industry workers, food technologists, and other careers.

What Do Food Industry Workers Do?

The first section of each chapter begins with a heading such as "What Dietitians and Nutritionists Do" or "What Winemakers Do." This section tells what it's like to work at this job. It describes typical responsibilities and assignments. You will find out about working conditions. Which workers are employed on farms? Which ones work at computers in offices? Which ones work in schools? This section answers these and other questions.

How Do I Become a Food Industry Worker?

The section called "Education and Training" tells you what schooling you need for employment in each job—a high school diploma, training at a junior college, a college degree, or more. It also talks about on-the-job training that you can expect to receive after you're hired, and whether or not you must complete an apprenticeship program.

How Much Do Food Industry Workers Earn?

The "Earnings" section gives salary figures for the job described in the chapter. These figures give you a general idea of how much money people with this job can make. Keep in mind that many people really earn more or less than the amounts given here because actual salaries depend on many different things, such as the size and location of the company and the amount of education, training, and experience you have. Generally, but not always, bigger companies located in major cities pay more than smaller ones in smaller cities and towns, and people with more education, training, and experience earn more. Also remember that these figures are current or recent salaries. They will probably be different by the time you are ready to enter the workforce.

What Is the Future of Food Careers?

The "Outlook" section discusses the employment outlook for the career. Here you will discover whether the total number of people employed in this career will increase or decrease in the coming years and whether jobs in this field will be easy or hard to find. These predictions are based on the economy, the size and makeup of the population, foreign competition, and new technology. This section uses terms such as "faster than the average," "about as fast as the average," and "slower than the average" to describe job growth. These terms and predictions are based on information from the U.S. Department of Labor.

Keep in mind that these predictions are general statements. No one knows for sure what the future will be like. Also remember that the employment outlook is a general statement about an industry and does not necessarily apply to everyone. A determined and talented person may be able to find a job in an industry or career with the worst outlook. And a person without ambition and the proper training will find it difficult to find a job in even a booming industry or career field.

Where Can I Find More Information?

Each chapter concludes with a "For More Info" section. It lists resources that you can contact to find out more about the field and careers in the field. You will find the names, addresses, phone numbers, and websites of food-oriented associations and organizations.

Extras

Every chapter has a few extras. There are photos that show food industry workers in action. There are sidebars and notes on ways to explore the field, fun facts, or lists of websites and books that might be helpful. At the end of the book you will find a glossary, index, and a "Browse and Learn More" section. The glossary gives brief definitions of words that relate to education, career training, or employment that you may be unfamiliar with. The index includes all the job titles mentioned in the book. The "Browse and Learn More" section lists general food-related books and websites to explore.

It's not too soon to think about your future. We hope you discover several possible career choices in the food industry. Have fun exploring!

Bakery Industry Workers

What Bakery Industry Workers Do

Bakery industry workers produce bread, cakes, pies, and other baked goods in commercial, institutional, and industrial bakeries.

Most bakery industry workers working for manufacturers (for example, a large company that produces hamburger buns or coffee cakes) participate in only some of the stages of baking. These workers, known as *food batchmakers,* are usually designated by the type of machine they operate or the stage of baking with which they are involved.

In preparing the dough or batter for goods baked in an industrial bakery, different workers make different components. *Blenders* tend machines that blend flour. Skilled technicians known as *broth mixers* control flour sifters and various vats to measure and mix liquid solutions for fermenting, oxidizing, and shortening. *Batter mixers* tend machines that mix ingredients for batters for cakes and other products. Other kinds of mixers and shapers include *unleavened-dough mixers, sweet-goods-machine operators,* and *pretzel twisters.*

Cracker-and-cookie-machine operators roll dough into sheets and form crackers or cookies before baking. *Wafer-machine operators* perform similar tasks with wafer batter. *Batter*

To Become a Successful Bakery Worker, You Should . . .

- ○ have good manual dexterity
- ○ have artistic ability if you are required to decorate cakes, cookies, doughnuts, and other baked goods
- ○ be able to work well as part of a team
- ○ have strong communication skills
- ○ have a keen sense of smell and taste

EXPLORING

○ Take baking or cooking classes that are offered locally by community centers, grocery stores, or tech schools.

○ Ask your teacher or parent to help arrange for a tour of a local bakery and talk to workers about their jobs.

○ If there is a cooking school in your area, visit it and meet with the teachers to discuss this line of work.

○ If you are in high school, you may be able to get a part-time or summer job at a neighborhood bakery. Although you may only be responsible for taking customers' orders and ringing up sales, you will be able to experience working in this environment.

scalers operate machines that deposit measured amounts of batter on conveyors. *Doughnut makers* and *doughnut-machine operators* mix batter, shape, and fry doughnuts.

Bakery helpers grease pans, move supplies, measure dump materials, and clean equipment. They may also fill, slice, package, seal, stack, or count baked goods.

When baked goods are ready for delivery and sale, *bakery checkers* distribute them to *route-sales drivers,* who deliver products to customers. Bakeries also employ *bakery-maintenance engineers,* also called *bakery-machine mechanics* or *plant mechanics,* to keep the many mixers, ovens, and other machines in good order.

Bread and pastry bakers, known as *pastry chefs,* also work in restaurants, small businesses such as the neighborhood bakeries, and institutions such as schools. Unlike bakery workers employed in industrial settings, these bakers and chefs often do much of their work by hand. They may have a fair amount of independence in deciding what items and how much of them to produce. Creativity is needed, especially when decorating an item made for a special occasion, such as a birthday cake or a wedding cake.

Education and Training

Most employers prefer to hire high school graduates. There are many high school classes that will help you prepare for this field. Family and consumer science will teach you about food preparation. Health classes will educate you about nutrition and sanitation. Math classes, such as algebra and geometry, will help you to become comfortable working with numbers and making calculations. You may also want to take science courses such as biology and chemistry to get an understanding of substances' properties and reactions. If you are interested in working as a bakery-maintenance engineer, take shop classes that will teach you to work with electricity and machinery.

Some bakery industry workers acquire useful skills through education in technical schools or in the U.S. Armed Forces. However, they usually complete their education on the job. In some companies, bakery workers can learn through formal apprenticeships.

A bakery industry worker at a supermarket displays a tray of pastries. (Ken Hammond, USDA)

Learn More about It

Beranbaum, Rose Levy. *The Bread Bible*. New York: W.W. Norton & Company, 2003.

Gisslen, Wayne. *Professional Baking*. 4th ed. Hoboken, N.J.: John Wiley & Sons, 2004.

Glezer, Maggie. *Artisan Baking across America: The Breads, the Bakers, the Best Recipes*. New York: Artisan Press, 2000.

Reinhart, Peter. *The Bread Baker's Apprentice: Mastering the Art of Extraordinary Bread*. Berkeley, Calif.: Ten Speed Press, 2001.

Shapter, Jennie, and Christine Ingram. *Bread Bakers Bible*. London, U.K.: Southwater Publishing, 2000.

Williamson, Sarah. *Bake the Best Ever Cookies!* Nashville, Tenn.: Williamson Publishing Company, 2001.

FOR MORE INFO

For industry information, contact
American Bakers Association
1350 I Street, NW, Suite 1290
Washington, DC 20005-3300
Tel: 202-789-0300
Email: info@americanbakers.org
http://www.americanbakers.org

For information on training, contact
American Institute of Baking
1213 Bakers Way
PO Box 3999
Manhattan, KS 66505-3999
Tel: 800-633-5137
Email: info@aibonline.org
http://www.aibonline.org

For industry information, contact
American Society of Baking
27 East Napa Street, Suite G
Sonoma, CA 95476
Tel: 707-935-0103
http://www.asbe.org

Apprenticeships consist of a blend of classroom and on-the-job instruction and take several years to complete.

Earnings

Salaries for bakery industry workers vary widely due to factors such as size and type of employer, the employee's experience, and job position. According to the U.S. Department of Labor, the median yearly earnings for all bakers were $20,990 in 2003. Salaries ranged from less than $14,390 to $34,580 or more.

Outlook

Employment for bakery industry workers will grow about as fast as the average over the next several years. The increasing use of automated equipment and processes will result in only fair employment opportunities in manufacturing. However, employment will be better for bakery workers at retail locations. Additionally, many positions will become available as workers retire or change jobs.

Beverage Industry Workers

What Beverage Industry Workers Do

Beverage industry workers manufacture and bottle soft drinks (including carbonated beverages), coffee, tea, juices, and more recently, mineral and spring waters.

The beverage industry provides jobs in many phases of manufacturing, from mixing syrups for soft drinks to working on assembly lines for bottling, sealing, shipping, distributing, and selling the products. Plant, distribution, and sales managers are a few of the administrative positions, while maintenance, shipping, and technical workers are employed by most companies. There are also many small companies involved at the bottling and wholesale level, where workers process, sell, and distribute beverages.

Plants that process soft drinks need workers to control flows, pressures, temperatures, line speeds, carbonation, Brix (measurement of sugar solution), and in-line blending.

Workers may be employed in growing and harvesting of beverage industry products, such as coffee, tea, citrus, and other fruits, as well as the processing, packaging, shipping, distribution, and selling of these products.

Since many teas and coffees are imported from other countries, workers are needed to import, process, package, ship, and distribute these

Interesting Website

Visit the following website to learn how Coca-Cola is made:

http://www.vpt.coca-cola.com/vpt_index.html

EXPLORING

○ Read industry publications and visit their websites to learn about new trends, terminology, and important manufacturers. *Beverage World* magazine (http://www.beverageworld.com), *Beverage Digest* newsletter (http://www.beverage-digest.com), and *Tea & Coffee Trade Journal* (http://www.teaandcoffee.net) are good publications to read.

○ Talk with a beverage industry worker about his or her career.

○ If you are a high school student, try to get a summer or part-time job at a manufacturing plant in your area. No matter what position you get, you'll have an inside look at the beverage industry. If there isn't a plant in your area, look for work in any setting related to the beverage industry, such as grocery stores, juice bars, coffee shops, and delivery services.

products as well as sell them. Beverage industry workers are also needed to create the sweeteners, syrups, bottles, cans, labels, and other items that support the manufacturing and sale of beverages.

In all areas of the beverage industry, positions range from unskilled laborers to highly paid administrative and sales staff. There also are many technical and scientific positions, where people work to create new types of beverages, new flavors, and new packaging, as well as oversee quality control. Still another area of employment related to the beverage industry is the recycling of cans and bottles.

Education and Training

A high school diploma is required for many positions in the beverage industry, but that is only the beginning of preparation for this work. Courses in family and consumer science, chemistry, shop, mathematics, and business will help prepare you for both the job itself and further training that is required in this complex and multilayered field.

Although there are almost always some positions available for unskilled laborers, it is unlikely that you will advance in this field if you have not earned at least a high school diploma. Much training is provided by beverage companies, but basic education is necessary to qualify for more sophisticated training programs.

Soft Drinks Facts

- The first cola-flavored beverage was produced in 1881.
- Nearly 450 different soft drinks are available in the United States.
- In 2003, the average American drank slightly more than 52 gallons of carbonated soft drinks.
- Of soft drinks consumed, approximately 77 percent are packaged and 23 percent dispensed from fountains.
- Less than 500 bottlers operate in the United States.
- More than 183,000 people are employed in the U.S. soft drink industry.

Source: American Beverage Association

If you want to work in a management, supervisory, or quality control position, you will need at the minimum a college degree. Typical majors for those working in these areas include the sciences (biology and chemistry), engineering, or business.

Earnings

Earnings for beverage industry workers vary based on their specific responsibilities, the size of their employer, the location, their union affiliation, their experience, and other factors. Those in management, supervisory, research and development, or engineering positions naturally tend to have higher earnings. In general, workers can expect the following salary ranges by specialty: quality control/assurance $25,000 to $50,000; maintenance, $25,000 to $60,000; and production, $10,700 to $50,000.

Outlook

New drink products enter the market each year, and during the past decade, specialty companies, such as Starbucks Coffee and

FOR MORE INFO

For information on soft drinks and other beverages, contact
American Beverage Association
1101 16th Street, NW
Washington, DC 20036
Tel: 202-463-6732
http://www.nsda.org

To learn more about the bottled water industry, water facts, and read news releases, visit the IBWA website.
International Bottled Water Association (IBWA)
1700 Diagonal Road, Suite 650
Alexandria, VA 22314
Tel: 703-683-5213
Email: ibwainfo@bottledwater.org
http://www.bottledwater.org

For information on education and links to related trade groups, visit the ISBT website.
International Society of Beverage Technologists (ISBT)
8110 South Suncoast Boulevard
Homosassa, FL 34446
Tel: 352-382-2008
Email: isbt@bevtech.org
http://www.bevtech.org

the many herbal tea manufacturers, have added millions of dollars and hundreds of jobs to the workplace. In addition to regular coffee, customers now can choose from espresso, café latte, hazelnut, mocha, and combinations of flavors. Energy drinks represent another growing area in the beverage industry. In addition to growth from new products, carbonated soft drinks, the old stand-bys, continue to dominate the U.S. beverage industry. The average American drinks gallons and gallons of soft drinks every year. As long as people are thirsty, there should be steady job opportunities in this field.

Brewers

What Brewers Do

Brewers oversee the production of beer, from selecting the exact blend and kind of flavoring hops to regulating the number of minutes the wort (liquid formed by soaking mash in hot water and fermenting it) boils. There are certain guidelines for each style of beer, but within those guidelines the brewer may experiment to create a truly unique flavor.

There are more than 50 styles of beer, but the four basic ingredients of all beers are malted barley, hops, yeast, and water. Brewers grind the malted barley in special machines so that its husk is removed and the kernel broken. Next, they add a precise amount of water and raise the temperature to dissolve the natural sugars, starches, and enzymes of the barley. To complete the mashing process, the brewer strains out the barley grains. The remaining sweetened liquid, called malt extract, is now ready to become the wort, which is concentrated, unhopped beer. The brewer transfers the wort from the mashing vessel to a brewing kettle, where boiling hops are added. The hopped wort is boiled, and after it has cooled, the hop leaves or pellet residue are removed in a process called sparging. The wort is now ready for its most vital ingredient, yeast. When the yeast is added, the fermentation process begins.

After the desired time for the primary fermentation, the brewer transfers the beer to a lagering kettle, where the beer is allowed to age. The

Did You Know?

○ Beer is one of the oldest alcoholic beverages known to humanity. It has been brewed for approximately 8,000 years.
○ Beer brewing in the United States began in the 1630s.
○ Ninety to 95 percent of beer is water.

EXPLORING

○ Although you cannot drink beer legally until you are 21 years old, you can learn more about the brewing of beer by visiting a micro-brewery, a brewpub, or one of the major mass-production breweries.

○ Read books and magazines on brewing beer. *Zymurgy,* the American Homebrewers Association's magazine, focuses on homebrewing issues. Visit http://www.beertown.org for a link to this publication.

○ If you're not of legal drinking age, you can still learn some of the basic skills of a brewer by making nonalcoholic carbonated drinks, such as sodas. Articles on this topic are frequently found in beer magazines because so much of the same equipment is used to make each.

fermentation continues but at a slower pace. After the desired aging or maturation of the beer (anywhere from two weeks to several months), the beer is again transferred to a storage tank, where it is ready to be bottled.

Brewers add carbonation to their beers either by injecting carbon dioxide into the storage tank just before the beer is to be bottled or kegged or by adding a priming sugar, usually dry malt extract or corn sugar diluted in boiled water.

Some *craftbrewers* at microbreweries may also help in bottling their beer. But a brewer's primary duty is always to brew beer, to experiment and come up with new recipes, and to seek out the right ingredients for the particular style of beer that is being brewed.

Most brewers are content to remain masterbrewer of a microbrewery or brewpub, but some may advance to management positions if the opportunity arises. *Brewery managers* are responsible for the day-to-day operations of a brewery, including managing finances, marketing, and hiring employees.

Education and Training

High school classes in biology, chemistry, and mathematics will be particularly useful if you are interested in becoming a brewer. Classes in biochemistry and microbiology will prepare you for the more specialized aspects of brewing that serious craftbrewers must master. You will need a background in science and mathematics to be able to perform basic brewing and engineering calculations and to follow technical discussions on brewing topics.

Employers today prefer to hire brewers who have completed some kind of formal training program in brewing sciences, or who have had extensive apprenticeship training at another brewery. See the sources at the end of this article for information on training programs. A college degree is not required for admission to the professional brewing programs, but you will need to complete college course work in biological sciences (biology, biochemistry, microbiology), chemistry, physics, mathematics (pre-calculus), and engineering.

Breweries of any size must be licensed both by the state in which they are located and the Bureau of Alcohol, Tobacco, Firearms, and Explosives. Owners of breweries are responsible for obtaining and maintaining these licenses. Brewers must be 21 years of age or older.

Earnings

Salaries for those in the brewing business vary considerably based on several factors, including the exact position a person holds, the size of the brewery, its location, the popularity of its beer, and the length of time the brewery has been in business. Brewers running their own microbreweries or brewpubs, like

To Be a Successful Brewer, You Should . . .

- ○ have an appreciation for beer and an excellent sense of taste
- ○ be able to distinguish between styles of beer
- ○ have strong organizational and problem-solving skills
- ○ have patience to allow beer to brew in its natural time
- ○ be able to follow recipes and procedures closely, but also have creativity to change a recipe or procedure to fix a problem during the brewing process or to improve the quality of a beer

FOR MORE INFO

For information on craftbrewing and apprenticeships, contact
American Brewers Guild
1001 Maple Street
Salisbury, VT 05769
Email: abg@abgbrew.com
http://www.abgbrew.com

For information on professional brewing and homebrewing and related publications, contact
Association of Brewers
736 Pearl Street
Boulder, CO 80302
Tel: 303-447-0816
http://www.beertown.org

For information on courses and the diploma in brewing technology, contact
Siebel Institute of Technology & World Brewing Academy
1777 North Clybourn Street, Suite 2F
Chicago, IL 60614-5520
Tel: 312-255-0705
Email: info@siebelinstitute.com
http://www.siebelinstitute.com

any small business owner, may have very low take-home wages for several years as the business becomes established. Earnings could possibly range from nothing to $20,000 or so. Head brewers and masterbrewers with a couple years of professional experience and working for a brewery may have earnings that range from $30,000 to $65,000.

Outlook

America is undergoing a beer renaissance. Beer can be as complex as wine and equally enjoyable. Major brewers such as Miller, Anheuser Busch, and Coors have acknowledged the craftbrewing trend by introducing their own premium-style beers. As people have become accustomed to the availability of unique tasting beers, they have created a growing market for these products. There is a strong demand for skilled brewers, and those with training should have the best opportunities.

Canning and Preserving Industry Workers

What Canning and Preserving Industry Workers Do

Canning and preserving industry workers monitor equipment and perform routine tasks in food-processing plants that can, preserve, and quick-freeze such foods as vegetables, fruits, frozen dinners, jams, jellies, preserves, pickles, and soups. They also process and preserve seafood, including shrimp, oysters, crabs, clams, and fish.

In large plants, each worker may perform one specific task. In smaller plants, one worker may perform many of the tasks necessary to preserve the food.

In order to operate successfully, a food-processing plant must have plenty of the foodstuffs it processes. Some of the major tasks performed by workers outside processing plants include negotiating with farmers to grow certain kinds of food crops for processing; bartering with farmers concerning price, the quantity that will be delivered, and the quality standards that the crop must meet; and purchasing raw materials and other goods for processing.

When food arrives at the processing plant, workers examine and

Facts about Frozen Food

○ The first frozen food products were created by Clarence Birdseye in the 1930s.

○ Ninety-four percent of shoppers purchase frozen food sometimes.

○ Frozen dinners/entrees are the most popular frozen food.

○ Approximately 1.5 million people are employed in the food manufacturing industry.

Source: American Frozen Food Institute, Tupperware Corporation, U.S. Department of Labor

17

record its quality, or grade, and mark it for separation by class, size, color, and condition. Then they unload it for processing.

Although most processing of food is done with automatic machines, workers are still needed to operate machinery; inspect, unload, sort, and wash food; measure ingredients, and monitor production processes. Plants that process fish and shellfish need workers to kill, prepare, and clean the fish before processing.

Next, foods are processed. They may be cooked, blanched (scalded with hot water or steam), deep-fried, pickled, smoked, frozen, or dehydrated. No matter the process, workers are needed to prepare food for these processes and operate equipment during the process.

Other foods, including many vegetables, are processed after they have been sealed in cans. Workers are needed to fill cans or jars with food to specified volume and weight and operate closing machines to put an airtight seal on the containers.

Once food has been processed and packaged, it is labeled, tested, and inspected. Workers test and inspect cans, jars, and other packaging to ensure that they are sealed correctly and do not contain foreign materials.

Managers of all types are needed to monitor and coordinate the activities of workers. They hire and fire employees, train workers, contact buyers, coordinate maintenance and operation of plant machinery, and meet with other managers to discuss production goals and other issues.

Education and Training

To prepare for this career, take high school classes in mathematics, science, family and consumer science, English,

EXPLORING

○ Ask your teacher or parent to arrange a tour of a food-processing plant in your area. Such a visit will give you a general overview of the jobs in the plant.

○ Talk to people employed in different jobs in canning or preserving plants. Ask them what they like and dislike about their jobs and why they entered the field.

○ If you are in high school, you may be able to get a part-time or summer job in a processing plant.

The Origins of Modern Canning

Nicolas Appert, a native of France, invented what we consider modern canning techniques in the late 1700s. During the Napoleonic Wars, more soldiers were falling ill or dying due to scurvy, malnutrition, and starvation than from enemy soldiers. To combat this problem, the French government offered a reward to the person who could find a way to preserve food. Appert, a brewer, baker, and candy-maker, experimented for 14 years until he realized that food could be preserved by putting it into bottles, corking them, and submerging them in boiling water. Voila! Food spoilage became much less of a problem, and Appert became a rich man due to his creativity and tenacity.

Source: National Food Processors Association

and computer science. Many food-processing jobs have no minimum educational requirements, although most employers prefer high school graduates; a high school diploma is essential for those seeking advancement. Beginners seldom need previous experience, and usually they can learn their jobs quickly. Generally there is up to one month of on-the-job training.

Many plants provide orientation sessions for new workers and programs on safety and sanitation. For those who aspire to management positions, a college degree is recommended, with studies in accounting, management, and other business courses as well as chemistry.

Some states require skilled and technical staff in plants to be licensed.

Earnings

Although some products can be processed at any time during the year, the level of activity in many food-processing plants varies with the season,

Cans are filled by a machine (left), then they pass through a closing machine (right). The filled cans are then weighed, cooked, labeled, and cased. (Campbell Soup)

and earnings of workers vary accordingly. Larger plants overcome the seasonality of their food products by maintaining large inventories of raw foodstuffs, and workers in these plants generally work full time throughout the year. Earnings for workers in the canning and preserving industry vary widely. Many positions, especially at the entry level, pay little more than the minimum wage. Experienced workers typically earn salaries that range from $20,000 to $30,000, while managers have earnings that range from $40,000 to $80,000 or more annually.

Outlook

The use of automated equipment and computer technology throughout the food-processing industry means that fewer people will be needed to process, preserve, and can foods. Wherever it is efficient and economical, machines will take over the tasks that people have been doing. Therefore, overall employment in the industry is expected to decline over the next several years. Researchers and technical workers with specialized expertise and college-level training will have the best employment opportunities.

FOR MORE INFO

For facts and statistics about frozen food, contact
American Frozen Food Institute
2000 Corporate Ridge, Suite 1000
McLean, VA 22102
Tel: 703-821-0770
Email: info@affi.com
http://www.affi.com

For information on careers and education, contact
Institute of Food Technologists
525 West Van Buren, Suite 1000
Chicago, IL 60607
Tel: 312-782-8424
Email: info@ift.org
http://www.ift.org

For information on the industry and safety issues and games for kids, contact
National Food Processors Association
1350 I Street, NW
Washington, DC 20005
Tel: 202-639-5900
Email: nfpa@nfpa-food.org
http://www.nfpa-food.org

Confectionery Industry Workers

What Confectionery Industry Workers Do

Confectionery industry workers manufacture and package sweets, including bonbons, hard and soft candy, stuffed dates, popcorn balls, and many other types of confections.

Confectionery industry workers operate machines to mix and cook candy ingredients, to form candy mixtures into shapes, and to package them for sale. Many different machines are used to make the molded, filled, pulled, whipped, and coated candies that Americans consume. Even when the candy-making production line is completely automated, workers still are needed to monitor the various processing steps. Some candy making jobs, especially in smaller candy factories, are still done by hand.

In some plants, *candy makers* are responsible for many of the steps in production, including formulating recipes and mixing, cooking, and forming candy. *Candy-maker helpers* help candy makers by tending machines, mixing ingredients, washing equipment, and performing other tasks. In large plants these jobs are

Chocolate Facts

- ○ Fifty-two percent of Americans cite chocolate as their favorite sweet snack.
- ○ Americans consume 11.7 pounds of chocolate per person each year.
- ○ The largest chocolate bar ever made weighed 5,025 pounds.
- ○ Halloween is the most popular holiday for candy sales. The next most popular holidays are Christmas and Valentine's Day.

Source: World Cocoa Foundation, National Confectioners Association

often performed by different workers, under the direction of *candy supervisors.* Plants also employ *factory helpers,* who move trays from machine to machine and help confectionery workers in other ways.

Education and Training

A high school diploma usually is required for employment in the confectionery industry. After they are hired, employees learn production skills on the job. High school courses in chemistry, biology, and shop are useful as background for some jobs, but skills are gained only through experience. Family and consumer science classes may offer you the opportunity to learn about cooking, baking, and food products. For some advanced positions, such as candy maker, workers may need technical expertise in food chemistry or other fields, as well as a solid knowledge of the industry.

For workers who want to advance to management positions, a bachelor's degree with an emphasis in food science technology and business courses is recommended.

Earnings

Confectionery workers' wages vary widely depending on such factors as the workers' skills and the size and location of the plant. According to the U.S. Department of Labor, weekly earnings for sugar and confectionery production workers averaged $597 in

EXPLORING

○ Try making candy at home. Fudge, taffy, candied apples, and chocolate covered pretzels are among the sweets you can make in your own kitchen.

○ Is there a candy manufacturing plant in your area? Call to see if tours are available.

○ If you are in high school, get a part-time or summer work at a candy store or the candy department of a large store where you can learn what products are popular, how the candy is stored and handled, and how to package it for customers.

○ If there is a candy manufacturer in your area, you may be able to get part-time or summer work as a helper while you are still in high school.

2002. This wage translates into a yearly income of approximately $31,044. Since this amount is the average, some workers make more than this salary and some workers make less. Entry-level, unskilled workers, such as helpers, may earn little more than the minimum wage, especially in smaller and nonunion factories. Those working full-time at the federal hourly minimum pay rate would have annual incomes of approximately $10,700.

Outlook

Candy sales in the United States are expected to hold about steady or perhaps increase slightly in coming years.

A confectionery industry worker inspects Hershey's Kisses as they move through the processing line. (Hershey Foods Corporation)

Facts about the Confectionery and Chocolate Industry

- ○ Four hundred companies manufacture more than **90** percent of confectionery and chocolate products in the United States.
- ○ Although candy is produced in 35 states, the candy industry is most active in Pennsylvania, New Jersey, Illinois, California, New York, Wisconsin, Texas, Virginia, and Ohio.
- ○ The industry employs approximately **65,000** workers.
- ○ To create its products, the industry annually uses 3 billion pounds of sugar, 635 million pounds of milk or milk products, 322 million pounds of domestic peanuts, 43 million pounds of California almonds, and 1.7 billion pounds of corn syrup sweeteners.

Source: Chocolate Manufacturers Association

FOR MORE INFO

For information on cocoa farming, producing chocolate, links to processing and manufacturing companies, and other helpful information, visit the CMA website.

Chocolate Manufacturers Association (CMA)
8320 Old Courthouse Road, Suite 300
Vienna, VA 22182
Tel: 703-790-5011
http://www.chocolateusa.org

For industry information, contact
National Confectioners Association (NCA)
8320 Old Courthouse Road, Suite 300
Vienna, VA 22182
Tel: 703-790-5750
Email: info@candyusa.com
http://www.ecandy.com

This website, sponsored by NCA and CMA, has information on candy history, quizzes, statistics, health news, and recipes.

Candy USA
http://www.candyusa.org

Candy making, however, has become increasingly automated. It is often possible to produce candy products from the raw materials to the finished, packaged product without that product having ever been touched by human hands. As more and more confectionery producers use automated machinery and equipment, the need for production workers, especially unskilled workers who do not have a college education, will decrease. In addition, the trend toward company consolidations will likely continue, meaning fewer employers of confectionery workers.

Most new openings will arise as workers change jobs. Large wholesale confectionery companies will provide the most employment opportunities.

Cookbook and Recipe Writers

What Cookbook and Recipe Writers Do

Cookbook writers may work as staff writers for a book publisher or may be self-employed. To write a cookbook, cookbook writers need to first decide what type of cookbook they would like to write. They then develop the various sections of the cookbook. They create a rough outline, which details the features (recipes, of course, but perhaps a glossary and other resources) that will be included in the book. Then they develop their recipe ideas. Recipes are a set of instructions that people use to prepare a food dish. Writers prepare each recipe many times to ensure that they have accurately presented measurements, portion sizes, ingredients, and any other component that may make or break a recipe. As they prepare the recipe, they take notes on the process for later review.

As they create and test the recipes, cookbook writers may also begin working on the other sections in the book. This allows them to tie in all of the various segments of the book so that they make sense to the readers. The table of contents details the various sections in the book. The introduction details the focus of the book

Did You Know?

○ The earliest known recipes appeared on Sumerian clay tablets and in Egyptian hieroglyphics.

○ The first cooking manuscripts were written by the ancient Greeks.

○ *American Cookery* was the first cookbook in the United States authored by an American. It was written by Amelia Simmons in 1796.

EXPLORING

○ Read books and visit websites about food and cooking.
○ Take cooking classes offered by your school or community organizations.
○ Try writing and preparing your own recipes. Be sure to take notes as you prepare each dish to help you determine what went right and what went wrong.
○ Ask your teacher or parent to arrange an information interview with a cookbook or recipe writer.

and, perhaps, the writer's personal reasons for writing the book. A how-to section gives the reader instructions on how to do a specific task, such as how to cut meat or dice vegetables The glossary contains definitions of cooking-related terms, and the bibliography lists other books and articles that the writer referred to as he or she wrote the book.

Recipe writers create recipes for books, magazines, newspapers, websites, and any other publication or product that features food-related articles and recipes. Recipes typically consist of the following components: the name of the dish, the amount of time needed to prepare the dish, the ingredients (usually listed in the order that they will be used), the equipment (stove, microwave, blender, baking pans, etc.), an ordered list of preparation instructions, and the number of servings the recipe will make. Recipe writers may also include information about the region or culture from which the recipe originated, nutritional information (including calories, fat content, etc.), and potential variations (such as a low-fat or low-carb version of the recipe) or substitutions (such as using skim milk instead of whole milk) that the reader may use when preparing the dish.

To create a useful recipe, recipe writers should explain every step, ingredient, and preparation process in detail, so that readers can prepare the recipe as easily as possible. They should also prepare their finished recipe many times to ensure that it contains no errors or confusing instructions.

Recipe writers also may work with food photographers, food stylists, food editors, and graphic designers. They work as freelance writers or as full-time employees at companies that publish recipes and related products.

Education and Training

If you are interested in becoming a cookbook and recipe writer, take English, general science, home economics, and computer classes while in high school. Writers must be expert communicators, so you should excel in English. Working on your school's newspaper, yearbook, or any other publication in high school will be useful.

Most cookbook and recipe writing jobs require a college education. Typical majors include English, communications, or culinary arts. You may wish to take cooking classes from a local culinary school or community college to enhance your marketability.

Earnings

According to the International Association of Culinary Professionals, cookbook authors typically earned $5,000 to $10,000 for their first book in 2002. Cookbook and recipe writers who worked on staff at a publication earned $19,000 to $40,000

On the Web

The Art of Writing Workable Recipes
http://www.stratsplace.com/rogov/art_writing_recipes.html

CooksRecipes.com
http://www.cooksrecipes.com

Food Network: Recipes
http://www.foodnetwork.com/food/recipes

Recipe Source
http://www.recipesource.com

FOR MORE INFO

This organization provides a wealth of industry information at its website.

International Association of Culinary Professionals
304 West Liberty Street, Suite 201
Louisville, KY 40202
Tel: 502-581-9786
Email: iacp@hqtrs.com
http://www.iacp.com

This organization offers an online newsletter and magazine at its website.

International Food, Wine & Travel Writers Association
PO Box 8249
Calabasas, CA 91372
Tel: 818-999-9959
http://www.ifwtwa.org

The following organization's website provides information on issues facing food writers and editors, such as ethics, spelling guidelines, and criticism guidelines.

Association of Food Journalists
http://www.afjonline.com

This website offers online courses and a newsletter on writing about food.

Food Writing
Email: editor@food-writing.com
http://www.food-writing.com

annually. Freelance food writers earned $100 to $1,000 per story. Salaries are generally higher in large cities. Salaries are also dependent on the employer, as larger publishers tend to pay more, and the writer's level of experience, as those with many years of experience are able to earn a larger salary.

Outlook

Employment opportunities for cookbook and recipe writers are expected to increase about as fast as the average over the next several years. Although Americans have a strong interest in food-related publications, aspiring cookbook and recipe writers will have a tough time breaking into this competitive field. However, cookbooks and other publications that feature recipes continue to grow in popularity, thus providing more opportunities for those who wish to pursue a career in food writing.

Cooking Instructors

What Cooking Instructors Do

Cooking instructors teach students at culinary and technical schools; private adult education enterprises; community colleges; middle, junior high, and high schools; and in any other setting where the art of cooking is taught. Students range from casual cooks to aspiring chefs who plan to make a career in the restaurant or food service industries.

Typical courses in a college-level culinary education program include mathematics; speech; economics; food history; food service; quantity food production; nutrition; food safety and sanitation; menu development; cost control; knife skills; purchasing; kitchen, employee, and restaurant management; computers in the food industry; ethics; wines and beverages; soups, stocks, and sauces; pastry; bread baking; meat identification and preparation; seafood identification and preparation; and foreign language (e.g., Spanish, French, or Italian). Other courses may teach students about regional, national, or international culinary styles and techniques. Some schools may offer course work relating to resume preparation and job interviewing.

Cooking instructors at the college level spend about 80 percent of their

Types of Cooking

Moist-heat methods
- ○ boiling
- ○ braising
- ○ simmering
- ○ steaming

Dry-heat methods
- ○ baking
- ○ barbecuing
- ○ broiling/grilling
- ○ frying
- ○ microwaving
- ○ roasting

EXPLORING

○ Watch cooking shows on television.
○ Take a cooking class to learn more about cooking and to observe a cooking instructor at work. Many cooking schools offer classes for young people.
○ Visit the websites of culinary schools to learn more about their educational programs. Visit http://www.culinary-art-schools.info for a list of schools.
○ Ask your teacher or parent to set up an information interview with a cooking instructor.
○ If you are in high school, talk to your home economics teacher about the career.

class time conducting hands-on instruction with students in lab kitchens. Some postsecondary institutions even feature working restaurants where students can sharpen their culinary skills by preparing and serving food to actual customers. Instructors spend the rest of their class time demonstrating culinary techniques, lecturing students, assigning readings and homework, and taking attendance. Outside of class, they prepare and administer lessons and exams and grade student work. They also meet with students individually to discuss class progress and grades.

Cooking instructors at the middle, junior high, and high school levels typically are known as *home economics teachers* or *family and consumer science teachers*. They teach students about basic nutrition, food safety and sanitation, and cooking techniques.

Education and Training

To prepare for a career as a cooking instructor, take high school courses in family and consumer science, English, mathematics, business, and science. Since many cooking terms are derived from the French language, you might want to take French. Other foreign languages that might be useful are Spanish and Italian.

Culinary arts institutions typically require teachers to have a minimum of a bachelor's degree in culinary arts and at least three years experience in the restaurant or food service industries.

To protect the public's health, chefs, cooks, and bakers are required by law in most states to possess a health certificate and to be examined periodically. These examinations, usually

*A cooking instructor at the California Culinary Academy teaches a young
student how to peel fruit.* (James A Sugar/Corbis)

given by the state board of health, make certain that the individual is free from communicable diseases and skin infections. Many employers require that new hires have certification in culinary education from the American Culinary Federation.

Elementary, middle, and secondary teachers who work in public schools must be licensed under regulations established by the state in which they are teaching.

To Be a Successful Cooking Instructor, You Should . . .

○ have comprehensive knowledge of culinary history, techniques, and cuisines
○ be well-organized
○ have good communication skills
○ be patient with students who may not master techniques as quickly as you would like
○ have well-developed senses of taste and smell
○ consider teaching a calling and have a strong desire to impart your knowledge to others
○ have at least three years experience in the restaurant or food service industries

FOR MORE INFO

For information on apprenticeships and culinary trends, contact
American Culinary Federation Inc.
180 Center Place Way
St. Augustine, FL 32095
Tel: 800-624-9458
Email: acf@acfchefs.net
http://www.acfchefs.org

For information on educational programs, including classes for kids, contact
Culinary Institute of America
1946 Campus Drive
Hyde Park, NY 12538-1499
Tel: 800-285-4627
http://www.ciachef.edu

Earnings

Earnings vary widely according to the number of courses taught, the instructor's experience, and the geographic region where the institution is located. Salaries for all postsecondary teachers ranged from less than $23,080 to $92,430 or more in 2002, according to the U.S. Department of Labor. Self-enrichment education teachers at junior colleges had mean annual earnings of $34,760 in 2003. Middle, junior high, and high school cooking instructors earn salaries that range from less than $25,000 to $70,000 or more annually.

Because many cooking instructors are employed part time, they are often paid by the hour or by the course, with no health insurance or other benefits. Hourly rates range from $6 to $50.

Outlook

Enrollments in culinary schools have surged in recent years, according to the Culinary Institute of America. This is good news for aspiring cooking instructors who will be needed to teach students interested in improving their culinary abilities or those planning to become cooks, chefs, or educators. Overall, faster than average growth is predicted for all postsecondary teachers over the next several years. Employment for middle, junior high, and high school teachers should grow about as fast as the average over the same time period.

Cooks and Chefs

What Cooks and Chefs Do

Cooks and *chefs* prepare and cook food in restaurants, hotels, cafeterias, and other eating places. They plan menus, order food, and measure and mix ingredients. They also cook and test the food and arrange it on plates. Some specialize in a certain area, such as cutting meat, boning fish, fixing sauces, or making salads, soups, or desserts.

Chefs may do many of these things, but their major job is to oversee all the activities in the kitchen. They also create recipes and train cooks. It is the responsibility of the chef to keep track of work schedules. Some chefs specialize in a particular cooking style, such as French or Italian.

Cooks and chefs may work a long week of 48 hours or more. This usually includes evening and weekend work because that is when many people eat in restaurants.

Successful cooks and chefs have a keen interest in food preparation and cooking and a desire to experiment in developing new recipes and new food combinations. They should be able to work as part of a team and to work under pressure during rush hours, in close quarters, and with a certain amount of noise and confusion. These employees need an even temperament and patience to contend with the public daily and to work closely with many other kinds of employees.

On the Web

KidsKuisine
http://www.kidskuisine.com

Nutrition Explorations
http://www.nutritionexplorations.org

Ultimate Cooking: The Young and the Edible
http://www.ultimatecooking.com/kidcook.htm

EXPLORING

○ Practice cooking for your family and friends. Ask relatives for recipes and also keep an eye out for them in magazines and on prepared food boxes, or you can create your own recipes.

○ Help your mom or dad prepare a meal.

○ Volunteer at a local kitchen that serves the homeless or others in need.

○ Ask your teacher to set up a presentation by a cook or chef.

Although cooks and chefs sometimes also bake, *bakers* specialize in preparing only baked goods, such as cakes, cookies, breads, and other treats. These are sold at bakeries, hotels, restaurants, cafeterias, and large food-chain stores.

Education and Training

Many cooks and chefs enter the profession through on-the-job training in restaurants or hotels. Although a high school education is not always required, it is essential for those who wish to move up to better jobs. In high school, you can prepare for a career as a cook or chef by taking classes in family and consumer science. Since many cooking terms are derived from the French language, courses in French and other languages should also be helpful.

The best job opportunities are available to those who graduate from special cooking schools or culinary institutes. These schools have classes in menu planning, food costs, purchasing, food storage, sanitation, health standards, and cooking and baking techniques. Graduates may have to serve as an apprentice or work in a supporting role before being hired as a cook or, some years down the road, head chef in a top restaurant or hotel.

Cooks and chefs are required by law in most states to possess a health certificate and to undergo a physical periodically. The American Culinary Federation offers certification at a variety of levels. While not always necessary, certification is a good idea if you want to advance your professional standing.

Employment for Cooks and Chefs

Career	Employment
Cooks, restaurant	727,000
Cooks, fast food	588,000
Cooks, institution and cafeteria	436,000
Cooks, short order	227,000
Chefs and head cooks	132,000
Cooks, private household	8,000

Source: U.S. Department of Labor, 2002

Earnings

Salaries for cooks and chefs vary widely based on many factors, such as the size, type, and location of the establishment, and the skill, experience, training, and specialization of the worker. Chefs and head cooks had median earnings of $28,750 in 2003, according to the U.S. Department of Labor. Salaries ranged from less than $16,310 to $54,420 or more. Restaurant cooks had median earnings of $19,260, and cooks working at institutions or cafeterias earned $18,300 a year. Cooks at fast food restaurants were at the bottom of the pay scale, earning $14,450 per year.

Cooks and chefs usually receive their meals free during working hours and are furnished with any necessary job uniforms. Those working full time usually receive standard benefits, such as health insurance and vacation and sick days.

Outlook

Overall, the employment of cooks and chefs is expected to increase about as fast as the average for all occupations over the next several years. Some careers, such as fast food cooks,

FOR MORE INFO

For information on apprenticeships and culinary trends, contact
American Culinary Federation Inc.
180 Center Place Way
St. Augustine, FL 32095
Tel: 800-624-9458
Email: acf@acfchefs.net
http://www.acfchefs.org

For information on educational programs contact
American Institute of Baking
1213 Bakers Way
PO Box 3999
Manhattan, KS 66505-3999
Tel: 785-537-4750
Email: info@aibonline.org
http://www.aibonline.org

For information on educational programs, including classes for kids, contact
Culinary Institute of America
1946 Campus Drive
Hyde Park, NY 12538-1499
Tel: 800-285-4627
http://www.ciachef.edu

may not see much growth in the number of new jobs because new, advanced machines require fewer people to operate them. However, turnover rates are high, and the need to find replacement cooks and chefs will mean many job opportunities in all areas. The need for cooks and chefs will also grow as the population increases and lifestyles change. As people make more money and have more leisure time, they dine out more often and take more vacations. In addition, working parents and their families dine out frequently as a convenience.

Dietitians and Nutritionists

What Dietitians and Nutritionists Do

Dietitians and *nutritionists* advise people on eating habits and plan diets that will improve or maintain their health. They work for themselves or for institutions such as hospitals, schools, restaurants, and hotels. *Registered dietitians* (RDs) have completed strict training and testing requirements designed by the American Dietetic Association. *Clinical dietitians* plan and supervise the preparation of diets designed for patients, and they work for hospitals and retirement homes. In many cases, patients cannot eat certain foods for medical reasons such as diabetes or liver failure. Dietitians see that these patients receive nourishing meals. They work closely with doctors, who advise them regarding their patients' health and the foods that the patients cannot eat.

Community dietitians usually work for clinics, government health programs, social service agencies, or similar organizations. They counsel individuals or advise the members of certain groups about nutritional problems, proper eating, and sensible grocery shopping.

Although most dietitians do some kind of teaching in the course of their work, *teaching dietitians* specialize in

It's a Fact

In the 18th century, French chemist Antoine-Laurent Lavoisier began to study the way the body uses food energy, or calories. He also studied the relationship between heat production and the use of energy. His work has caused him to be known as the "father of nutrition."

education. They usually work for hospitals, and they may teach full time or part time. Sometimes, teaching dietitians also perform other tasks, such as running a food service operation, especially in small colleges.

Consultant dietitians work with schools, restaurants, grocery-store chains, manufacturers of food service equipment, drug companies, and private companies of various kinds. Some consultants work with athletes and sports teams.

Research dietitians work for government organizations, universities, hospitals, drug companies, and manufacturers. They try to improve existing food products or find alternatives to unhealthy foods.

Nutritionists are people with various levels of training and skills. Regulations covering the use of this title vary from state to state. *Certified clinical nutritionists* (CCNs) have the same core educational and internship backgrounds as RDs but are specialists who have completed some postgraduate education that focuses on the biochemical and physiological aspects of nutrition science. CCNs typically work in private practice for themselves, as part of a group of health care professionals, or for a doctor or doctors in private practice. They work with clients to correct imbalances in the clients' biochemistry and improve their physiological function.

Education and Training

There are no specific educational requirements for nutritionists who are not dietitians, but most nutritionists have at least two years of college-level

EXPLORING

○ Read books about healthy diet and nutrition. Many cookbooks that feature healthy recipes have sections on nutrition.

○ Start collecting healthy recipes.

○ Do your own grocery shopping, and learn to pick out the best produce, meats, fish, and other ingredients.

○ Take cooking classes offered by your school and other organizations in your community. Supermarkets, for example, frequently offer classes on topics such as how to prepare low-cholesterol meals.

○ Prepare a healthy meal for your family once a week.

training in nutrition, food service, or another related subject.

To become a registered dietitian, you must have a bachelor's degree, complete a practice program that takes six to 12 months, and pass an examination. After that, you must complete continuing-education courses so that you can stay registered.

To be eligible for many positions in institutions, you must be an RD, a CCN, or a registered dietetic technician. If you want to teach, do research, or work in the field of public health, you will need one or more advanced degrees.

Currently 45 states have laws that require dietitians and nutritionists be licensed, certified, or registered.

An assistant samples a new low-carotene lunch that was prepared by a dietitian (right). (Keith Weller, USDA)

Earnings

The median annual salary for dietitians and nutritionists was $42,030 in 2003, according to the U.S. Department of Labor.

FOR MORE INFO

For comprehensive information on careers in dietetics, contact
American Dietetic Association
120 South Riverside Plaza, Suite 2000
Chicago, IL 60606-6995
Tel: 800-877-1600
http://www.eatright.org

For information on educational requirements and careers, contact
American Society for Nutritional Sciences
9650 Rockville Pike, Suite 4500
Bethesda, MD 20814
Tel: 301-634-7050
Email: sec@asns.org
http://www.asns.org

What Dietetic Technicians Do

Dietetic technicians work in two areas: food service management and nutrition care of individuals, also known as clinical nutrition. They usually work on a team, under the direction of a dietitian. Most technicians work for hospitals and nursing homes. Some, however, work for health agencies such as public health departments or neighborhood health centers.

Technicians in food service management work in kitchens, overseeing the actual food preparation. Some supervise *dietetic aides* who serve food to patients in the cafeteria and in their hospital rooms.

Technicians in clinical nutrition work under the supervision of a dietitian. They interview patients about their eating habits and the foods they like. They give this information to the dietitian, along with reports on each patient's progress. Technicians teach patients and their families about good nutrition.

Dietetic technicians must have a high school diploma and complete a two-year associate's degree program approved by the American Dietetic Association.

Beginning technicians earn between $14,000 and $20,000 a year. Workers with 10 to 15 years of experience may earn between $20,000 and $29,000 a year. Those at the top of the pay scale earn between $30,000 and $40,000.

The outlook for dietetic technicians for the next several years, especially for those who are certified, is good.

The lowest paid 10 percent earned less than $26,290; the highest paid 10 percent earned $60,540 or more a year.

Outlook

Employment of dietitians and nutritionists is expected to grow about as fast as the average over the next several years. The public is increasingly aware of the importance of nutrition, and people are consulting with experts for nutritional advice.

Family and Consumer Scientists

What Family and Consumer Scientists Do

Family and consumer scientists are concerned with the well-being of the home and family. They work in education, dietetics, research, social welfare, extension services, and business. Whatever the job, family and consumer scientists rely on their understanding of food and nutrition, child development, household management, and the many other elements involved in day-to-day living.

Family and consumer scientists who work as teachers in junior and senior high schools teach courses such as nutrition, clothing, cooking, child development, family relations, and home management. Teachers at the college level prepare students for careers in home economics. They also conduct research and write articles and textbooks.

Extension-service family and consumer scientists are part of an educational system supported by government agencies to educate and advise families, both rural and urban, on family life, nutrition, child care, and other aspects

Typical College Courses for Family and Consumer Science Majors

- Basic Nutrition
- Human Development
- Child Development
- Marriage and the Family
- Family Financial Management
- Nutrition in the Life Cycle
- Consumer Economics
- Apparel Production
- Apparel Merchandising
- Meal Management
- Food Science

Source: CollegeBoard.com

of homemaking. These scientists offer help and advice over the phone and may also travel to various communities to give presentations and provide assistance.

Health and welfare agencies hire family and consumer scientists to work with social workers, nurses, and physicians. They consult with low-income families who need help with financial management concerns. They develop community programs in health and nutrition, money management, and child care.

The business world offers many opportunities to family and consumer scientists. Some work for manufacturers, where they test and improve products and recipes and prepare booklets on uses of products. They plan educational programs and materials.

Family and consumer scientists who work in media and advertising agencies write about food, fashion, home decor, budgets, and home management. Those who work for retail stores help customers choose furniture and other household items and also work in advertising, buying, and merchandising.

Some family and consumer scientists specialize in dietetics. They work in hospitals, hotels, restaurants, or schools. They plan meals, order food and supervise its preparation, handle budgets, and plan special diets.

Family and consumer scientists who work as *researchers* create products and develop procedures that make life better for families. Researchers work for colleges and universities, government and private agencies, and private companies.

Education and Training

In high school, take courses in English, mathematics, foreign language,

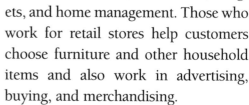

EXPLORING

○ Take home economics classes. These will teach you the basics of cooking, sewing, and home management.

○ Use your library and Internet resources to learn all you can about areas of family and consumer science that interest you, such as nutrition, child care, or consumer trends.

○ Your community 4-H club may offer opportunities in community service, arts, consumer and family sciences, environmental education, and healthy lifestyle education. Visit http://www.4h-usa.org for more information.

and history. You should also take any classes related to home economics, including child development, adult living, and health.

Family and consumer scientists must have at least a bachelor's degree in family and consumer science or home economics. Many colleges and universities offer these degrees, as well as specialization in subjects such as education, child development, food and nutrition, dietetics, institution management, textiles and clothing, family economics and home management, household equipment and furnishings, and applied art. Those who conduct research and teach college usually need a master's degree or a doctorate.

The American Association of Family and Consumer Sciences offers a voluntary certification program for professionals who have a bachelor's degree and who pass an examination. To teach elementary or secondary school classes, you must be licensed under regulations established by your state's department of education.

Earnings

Earnings among family and consumer scientists vary a great deal, depending on experience, education, and area of work. Those in entry-level positions, such as salespeople and child care workers, may have annual earnings of well below $20,000.

To Be a Successful Family and Consumer Scientist Who Specializes in Education, You Should . . .

- have respect for your students and be dedicated to their future success
- be patient
- be organized
- be self-confident in order to speak effectively before students of all ages
- have strong communication skills—both written and oral
- enjoy keeping up-to-date regarding new trends in family and consumer science

FOR MORE INFO

To order the career brochure Family and Consumer Sciences: Today's Profession Offering Tomorrow's Careers, *contact*
American Association of Family and Consumer Sciences
1555 King Street
Alexandria, VA 22314
Tel: 703-706-4600
Email: staff@aafcs.org
http://www.aafcs.org

But teachers and those in upper-level sales and marketing jobs can earn considerably more. The U.S. Department of Labor reports the following median salaries for teachers in 2003 by educational level: elementary, $42,160; middle, $42,450; and secondary, $44,580. College home economics teachers had median annual earnings of $48,690 in 2003, according to the U.S. Department of Labor. Food scientists earned an average of $49,510 a year in 2003.

Benefits such as health insurance, vacation, and sick leave vary by employer. Family and consumer scientists who go into teaching will most certainly enjoy the usual fringe benefits of the profession, including paid sick leave, group insurance, and retirement plans, as well as having two to three months free each year for travel, further study, or other professional enrichment.

Outlook

The demand for family and consumer scientists will be highest for specialists in marketing, merchandising, family and consumer resource management, food service and institutional management, food science and human nutrition, environment and shelter, and textiles and clothing. Also, with the elderly population growing, family and consumer scientists will be actively involved in social services, gerontology, home health care, adult day care services, and other programs that improve the quality of life for older people.

Those interested in teaching will find more opportunities at the elementary and secondary level than at the college level. Vocational education programs, youth pregnancy prevention, and at-risk youth are priorities for teachers and administrators.

Farmers

What Farmers Do

Farmers grow crops, such as peanuts, corn, wheat, cotton, fruits, or vegetables. They also raise cattle, pigs, sheep, chickens, and turkeys for food and keep herds of dairy cattle for milk. Throughout the early history of the United States, farming was a family affair. Today, however, family farms are disappearing. Most large farms are now run by agricultural corporations.

Farmers need good soil and a lot of water for their crops and animals. They need to know how to bring water to their plants (irrigation) and add rich nutrients (fertilizer) to the soil. They also need to know how to keep their animals and crops healthy. They must control insects and diseases that will damage or destroy crops or livestock. They also must provide proper care, such as clean, warm shelters, proper food, and special breeding programs.

Livestock farmers buy calves from ranchers who breed and raise them. They feed and fatten young cattle and often raise their own corn and hay to lower feeding costs. They need to be

Farming Facts

- In colonial America, almost 95 percent of the population were farmers. They planted corn, wheat, flax, and tobacco. Livestock, including hogs, cattle, sheep, and goats, were imported from Europe. Farmers raised hay to feed livestock and just enough other crops to supply their families with a balanced diet throughout the year.
- Over one-half of the world's population is still engaged in farming today.
- In the United States, farm employment dropped from 9.9 million in 1950 to 1.4 million in 2002.

familiar with cattle diseases and proper methods of feeding. They provide their cattle with fenced pasturage and adequate shelter from rough weather. *Sheep ranchers* raise sheep primarily for their wool. Large herds are maintained on rangeland in the western states. *Dairy farmers* are mostly concerned with producing high-grade milk, but they also raise corn and grain to feed their animals. Dairy animals must be milked twice each day. Farmers clean stalls and barns by washing, sweeping, and sterilizing milking equipment with boiling water. *Poultry farmers* usually do not hatch their own chicks but buy them from commercial hatcheries. The primary duty of poultry farmers is to keep their flocks healthy. They provide shelter from the chickens' natural enemies and from extreme weather conditions. The shelters are kept extremely clean, because diseases can spread through a flock rapidly. Some poultry farmers raise chickens to be sold as broilers or fryers. Others specialize in the production of eggs. *Beekeepers* set up and manage bee hives. They harvest and sell honey and also cultivate bees for lease to farmers to help pollinate their crops.

EXPLORING

Organizations such as 4-H and the National Future Farmers of America offer good opportunities for learning about, visiting, and participating in farming activities.

4-H Clubs
1400 Independence Avenue, SW
Washington, DC 20250-2225
http://www.4h-usa.org

National Future Farmers of America
6060 FFA Drive
PO Box 68960
Indianapolis, IN 46268-0960
http://www.ffa.org

Education and Training

Courses in mathematics and science, especially chemistry, earth science, and botany, are important for a career in farming. Accounting, bookkeeping, and computer courses are also very helpful.

After high school, enroll in either a two-year or a four-year course of study in a college of agriculture. For a person with no farm experience, a bachelor's degree in agriculture is essential.

Mmmm Good!

What do livestock eat? Animals need basic nutrients, such as proteins, carbohydrates, fats, minerals, and vitamins. Specially prepared feeds and roughage, such as hay, supply farm animals with these nutrients. Here's what goes into animal feeds:

○ pasturage (growing grasses, alfalfa, clover)

○ grains

○ hay

○ silage (pasturage and grains stored in airtight structures called silos and allowed to ferment)

○ high-protein concentrates (soybean meal, cottonseed oil, blood meal, and bone meal)

○ high-carbohydrate concentrates (corn, sorghum, molasses, and dehydrated potatoes)

○ food additives (hormones, antibiotics, vitamins, and minerals)

○ by-products from packinghouses, fruit and vegetable processing plants, breweries, distilleries, and paper mills

Some universities offer advanced studies in horticulture, animal science, agronomy, and agricultural economics. Most students in agricultural colleges also take courses in farm management, business, finance, and economics.

Farm operators can obtain voluntary certification as an accredited farm manager from the American Society of Farm Managers and Rural Appraisers.

Earnings

Farmers' incomes change from year to year depending on weather, the condition of their farm machinery, the demand for their crops and livestock, and the costs of feed, land, and equipment. According to the U.S. Department of Labor, farm managers had median annual earnings of $47,940 in 2003. Earnings ranged from less than $26,780 to $83,520 or more. Most farmers,

Two farmers in Raymondsville, Texas, examine freshly picked watermelon. (Ken Hammond, USDA)

especially those running small farms, earn incomes from nonfarm activities that may be several times larger than their farm incomes.

Outlook

Because farming is such a risky business, those entering the career cannot make it without family support or financial aid. Reports show that the number of farmers or farm laborers is decreasing. Rising costs and the trend toward larger farms are forcing out small farmers.

Despite the great difficulty in becoming a farmer today, there are many agriculture-related careers that involve people with farm production, marketing, management, and agribusiness.

FOR MORE INFO

The Farm Bureau hosts youth conferences and other events for those interested in farming.
American Farm Bureau Federation
600 Maryland Avenue, SW, Suite 800
Washington, DC 20024
Tel: 202-406-3600
http://www.fb.org

For information on farm policies, education, and other news relating to the agricultural industry, visit the USDA website.
U.S. Department of Agriculture (USDA)
1400 Independence Avenue, SW
Washington, DC 20250
Tel: 202-720-2791
http://www.usda.gov

Fishers

What Fishers Do

Fishers catch fish and other sea life and sell it to restaurants, fish markets, and other businesses. The various kinds of fishers are grouped according to the type of equipment they use, the type of fish they catch, and where they catch the fish.

Some fishers work alone in small boats and some work on crews of as many as 25 people in a group of boats called a fleet. They can remain at sea for several days or for months at a time. Most commercial fishing is done in ocean waters far from home port. Only a small percentage of fish are caught in rivers, streams, ponds, or lakes, or harvested from fish farms.

Fishers who catch fish with nets are called *net fishers*. They make up the largest group of fishers and catch most of the world's supply of fish. They use three main types of nets: seines, trawls, and gill nets. Fishing crews use seines to catch schools of herring, mackerel, sardines, tuna, and other fish that swim near the surface of the ocean. In funnel-shaped nets called trawls, fishers catch shrimp, cod, scallops, and other shellfish living on or near the ocean floor. Before they drop these nets, they use sonar to find where the greatest number of fish are located. Only a small number of fishers use the third type of net, the gill net. This net, which acts like

Did You Know?

○ Fishers hold approximately 36,000 jobs in the United States.

○ Approximately 50 percent of fishers are self employed—one of the highest percentages of all careers in the United States.

○ States that have the highest volume of caught fish include Alaska, Louisiana, Virginia, California, and Washington.

Source: U.S. Department of Labor

EXPLORING

○ Look for opportunities to go out on a fishing boat.

○ Contact a state department of fish and game to learn more about the local fishing industry.

○ If you don't live near the water, you can learn about saltwater fish by working for a pet shop or a state aquarium.

○ Working at a fish market can acquaint you with different kinds of fish and consumer demand for seafood.

a wall, entangles fish such as salmon, sharks, and herring.

Line fishers catch fish with poles, hooks, and lines. This takes a very long time. Line fishers work alone or in crews. They lay out lines and attach hooks, bait, and other equipment, depending on the type of fish they plan to catch. To haul catches on board they use reels, winches, or their bare hands.

Pot fishers trap crab, lobster, and eel in cages containing bait. Some chase turtles and certain kinds of fish into net traps. Pot fishing is done by lowering the cages into the water, pulling them in when the fish is trapped, and dumping the catch onto the deck. Pot fishers often sell their catches live to processors who can freeze the catches or sell them fresh.

Some fishers are primarily involved with recreational fishing. They operate fishing vessels for sport fishing, socializing, and relaxation.

Education and Training

Generally, fishers learn their trade on the job. But some high schools, colleges, and technical schools offer courses in handling boats, fishing equipment, navigation, and meteorology. These provide good preparation for a job in fishing. Short-term courses offered by postsecondary schools provide information on electronic navigation and communications equipment and the latest improvements in fishing gear.

Captains and first mates on large fishing vessels of at least 200 gross tons must be licensed. Captains of charter sport fishing boats must also be licensed, regardless of the size of the vessel.

Earnings

The income of commercial fishers varies widely. It changes according to the seasons, the amount of fish available, what people want to buy, and the skills and dedication of the fisher. Usually, fishers cannot count on a fixed salary. Instead, they earn a percentage of the catch or an hourly wage. But they can increase their earnings by working faster, improving their skills, and learning all they can about the fishing industry. In New England, ship owners can receive 50 percent of the catch's receipts. The captain may receive 10 percent, and the captain and crew share the remaining 40 percent. According to the Alaska Department of Fish and Game, a crew member receiving 6 to 15 percent of the net profit can earn between nothing and tens of thousands of dollars a year. According to the U.S. Department of Labor, fishers earn between $300 and $700 a week.

Outlook

The fishing industry has experienced hard times in the past few decades, and employment for fishers is expected to decline over the next several years. The industry is affected by environmental law, ship maintenance costs, improvements in electronic and other fishing gear (which has limited the expansion

U.S. Fisheries on the Rebound?

Although overfishing and pollution have decreased fish stocks throughout the world, there is some good news regarding U.S. fisheries. Thanks to efforts by NOAA Fisheries to help restore depleted stocks and rebuild ecosystems, U.S. fisheries may be on the rebound. In fact, in 2003:

○ Four fish stocks were completely restored.

○ A record 10 species were removed from the list of overfished species.

○ Overfishing practices were halted for five species.

Source: National Marine Fisheries Service

in crew size), and the increasing use of "floating processors," which process catches on-board, further limiting employment opportunities.

Pollution and excessive fishing have decreased the fish stock, particularly in the North Atlantic and Pacific Northwest. Some states have limited the number of fishing permits to allow regrowth of fish and shellfish populations.

FOR MORE INFO

Visit the Alaska Department of Fish and Game website to learn more about commercial fishing, harvest statistics, and commercial fishing seasons.

Alaska Department of Fish and Game
Division of Commercial Fisheries
PO Box 25526
Juneau, AK 99802-5526
Tel: 907-465-4210
http://www.state.ak.us/adfg

The NMFS's goals include building and maintaining sustainable fisheries. Visit its website for news, to sign up for the email newsletter FishNews, *and to read the online brochure* Celebrating American Seafood.

National Marine Fisheries Service (NMFS)

NOAA Fisheries Headquarters
1315 East-West Highway, 9th Floor F/CS
Silver Spring, MD 20910
http://www.nmfs.noaa.gov

This agency conducts research and provides information on the global oceans, atmosphere, space, and sun. It oversees the NMFS. Visit NOAA's website for news, statistics, and other information relating to fisheries.

National Oceanic and Atmospheric Administration (NOAA)
14th Street and Constitution Avenue, NW, Room 6217
Washington, DC 20230
Tel: 202-482-6090
http://www.noaa.gov

Food Service Workers

What Food Service Workers Do

Food service workers keep kitchens and dishes clean and help cooks prepare food. *Waiters, servers,* and *lunchroom or coffee shop counter attendants* take customers' orders, serve food and beverages, calculate bills, and collect money. Between serving customers, they clear and clean tables and counters, replenish supplies, and set up table service for future customers.

Some food service workers assist with food preparation. They gather the food and utensils and set up the pots and pans and other cooking equipment. They wash fruits and vegetables and chop ingredients for salads, sandwiches, or vegetable dishes. They mix ingredients, make coffee and tea, cook french fries, and do other tasks according to the cook's instructions.

Counter attendants also do some simple cooking tasks, such as making sandwiches, salads, and cold drinks and preparing ice cream dishes. They take customers' orders, fill them, and take payment at a cash register. They also may have to help clean kitchen equipment, sweep and mop floors, and carry out trash.

Waiters in full-service restaurants seat customers, present menus, suggest choices from the menu, and inform the customers of special preparations and seasonings of food. They take care of special requests and check each order to make sure it is correct before bringing it to the table.

Where Are Food Service Workers Employed?

- grills
- sandwich shops
- cafés
- soda shops
- diners
- large restaurants
- hotels
- cruise ships
- trains
- hospitals
- schools
- factories
- malls
- museums

EXPLORING

○ Take cooking classes and practice cooking for and serving your family.

○ Volunteer for food service jobs with community centers, shelters, and social-service agencies that serve meals to the needy.

○ Get a part-time or summer job as a dining room attendant, counter worker, or waiter at a restaurant, grill, or coffee shop with a casual atmosphere.

○ Dealing with the public is a large aspect of food service work, so get experience in this area. If you can't find employment in food service, look for work as a store clerk, cashier, or customer service worker.

Dining room attendants, also known as *waiters' assistants, buspersons,* or *bussers,* clear and reset tables, carry dirty dishes to the dishwashing area, carry in trays of food, and clean up spilled food and broken dishes. In some restaurants, these attendants also serve water and bread and butter to customers. They fill salt and pepper shakers, clean coffeepots, and do various other tasks.

Other food service workers scrape plates and load dishes in a dishwasher or wash them by hand. They clean the kitchen worktables, stoves, pots and pans, and other equipment. They sweep and mop the kitchen floor and throw away garbage. These workers are known as *kitchen assistants.*

Education and Training

You do not need to obtain any special education or training to work in an entry-level food service position. Training takes place on the job, so it is not always necessary to finish high school. However, classes in home economics, cooking, mathematics, and science are helpful. Food servers with experience can find better positions and higher tips at fine dining establishments. Some vocational schools offer training courses for waiters.

If you want to own or manage a restaurant, a high school diploma and additional study at a two- or four-year college of hotel or restaurant management is recommended.

Food service workers almost always are required to obtain health certificates from the state Department of Public Health that certify they are free from communicable diseases, as shown by physical examination and blood tests. This is required for the protection of the general public.

Earnings

Food service workers' earnings are determined by a number of factors, such as the type, size, and location of the food establishment, union membership, experience and training, basic wages, and in some cases, tips earned. Estimating the average wage scale therefore is difficult.

Most waiters depend on tips to supplement their hourly wages. According to the U.S. Department of Labor, waiters earned an average of $14,100 annually in 2003, including tips. Full-time dining room attendants earned an average annual salary of $14,570. Food counter workers earned median annual salaries of

Food service workers at a high school prepare peaches for a school lunch program. (Ken Hammond, USDA)

Learn More about It

Dahmer, Sondra J., and Kurt W. Kahl. *Restaurant Service Basics.* New York: John Wiley & Sons, 2001.

Kirkham, Mike, Peggy Weiss, and Bill Crawford. *The Waiting Game: The Ultimate Guide to Waiting Tables.* Austin, Tex.: Twenty Per Cent, LLC, 2000.

Sanders, Edward E., Paul Paz, and Ron Wilkinson. *Service at Its Best: Waiter-Waitress Training.* Upper Saddle River, N.J.: Prentice Hall, 2002.

FOR MORE INFO

For information on accredited education programs, contact

International Council on Hotel, Restaurant, and Institutional Education
2613 North Parham Road, 2nd Floor
Richmond, VA 23294
Tel: 804-346-4800
Email: info@chrie.org
http://chrie.org

For information on education and careers, contact

National Restaurant Association Educational Foundation
175 West Jackson Boulevard,
Suite 1500
Chicago, IL 60604-2814
Tel: 800-765-2122
Email: info@nraef.org
http://www.nraef.org

$15,360, and dishwashers earned $14,990.

Outlook

The overall employment outlook for those in food service should be about as fast as the average over the next several years. Many job openings will come from the need to replace workers who have left the field. Turnover is high in these jobs because of the low pay, the long hours, and the large number of students and others who do this work on a temporary basis before moving on to other occupations.

Food Technologists

What Food Technologists Do

Food technologists study the ways that foods are processed, preserved, and packaged. They look for ways to improve the flavor, appearance, nutritional value, and convenience of food products. They also perform tests to make sure that products meet quality standards.

Food technologists usually specialize in one phase of the food industry. Food technologists in basic research study the physical and chemical composition of foods and observe the changes that take place during storage or processing. This research helps them understand what factors affect the flavor, appearance, or texture of foods. Other technologists create new food products and develop new processing methods. They may also work with existing foods to make them more nutritious and flavorful and to improve their color and texture.

A rapidly growing area of food technology is biotechnology. Food technologists in this area work with plant breeding, gene splicing, microbial fermentation, and plant cell tissue cultures to produce enhanced raw products for processing.

Food technologists conduct chemical tests on products to be sure that food meets standards set by the government and by the food industry. They also determine the nutritive content (amounts of sugar, starch,

Did You Know?

○ There are 76 million cases of food-borne disease in the United States each year.

○ Approximately 325,000 of these cases require hospitalization.

○ Five thousand people die each year from food-borne disease.

Source: Centers for Disease Control and Prevention

EXPLORING

○ Develop your interests in cooking, and experiment with inventing your own recipes.

○ Chemistry is an important part of food technology, so participate in science clubs that allow you to explore chemical processes.

○ Tour local food processing plants to see how food is produced and packaged on a large scale.

○ Talk with a food technologist about his or her career.

protein, fat, vitamins, and minerals) in the product so that this information may be printed on the labels.

Some food technologists work in quality-control laboratories, where they concentrate on making sure that foods in every stage of processing meet industry and government standards. They check to see that raw ingredients are fresh and suitable for processing. They also test bacteria levels in foods after processing.

In processing plants, food technologists make sure that proper temperature and humidity levels are maintained in storage areas, wastes are disposed of properly, and other sanitary regulations are observed.

Some food technologists test new products in test kitchens or develop new processing methods in laboratory pilot plants. Others devise new methods for packaging and storing foods. They consult with processing engineers, flavor experts, and packaging and marketing specialists.

Food technologists work in laboratories, offices, and test kitchens and on production lines at food processing plants, food ingredient plants, and food manufacturing plants. Most are employed in private industry, but some work for government agencies, such as the Environmental Protection Agency, the Food and Drug Administration, and the U.S. Department of Agriculture.

Education and Training

Food technologists need at least a bachelor's degree in food technology, food science, or food engineering. Some technologists hold degrees in chemistry, biology, engineering, agriculture, or business. Master's degrees and doctorates are usually necessary for jobs in management or for research and teaching positions.

Undergraduate programs in food technology usually include courses in physics, biochemistry, mathematics, biology, the social sciences, humanities, and business administration in addition to food technology courses, such as food preservation, processing, sanitation, and marketing.

Earnings

Food technologists earned annual median salaries of $49,510 in 2003. Salaries ranged from less than $28,740 to $86,890 or more. Most food technologists receive generous benefit plans, which usually include health insurance, life insurance, pension plans, and vacation and sick pay. Others may receive funds for continuing education.

Outlook

The food industry is the single largest industry in the United States and throughout the world. In developed countries, consumer demand for new and different food products will create a demand for food scientists and technologists.

Words to Learn

food-borne illness　sickness resulting from eating food that is contaminated by bacteria, viruses, parasites, amoebas, and other biological and chemical agents

microorganism　a microscopic animal or plant-like organism

pasteurization　process in which food is heated under controlled conditions to destroy pathogenic microorganisms

pathogen　a microorganism that is capable of causing disease

sterilization　a process in food production where all harmful life forms (bacteria, viruses, etc.) are destroyed

Source: Institute of Food Technologists

Several factors have also created continuing demand for skilled technologists. Labeling laws require companies to provide detailed nutritional information on their products. The trend toward more healthful eating habits has encouraged companies to hire food technologists to create a variety of low-fat, low-carb, low-sodium, fat-free, cholesterol-free, and sodium-free foods.

Food technologists will also be sought to produce new foods for poor and starving people in underdeveloped countries. Experienced technologists will use their advanced training to create new foods from such staples as rice, corn, wheat, and soybeans.

FOR MORE INFO

For information on accredited food science programs and to read Introduction to the Food Industry, visit the Continuing Education & Professional Development section of the IFT website.
Institute of Food Technologists (IFT)
525 West Van Buren, Suite 1000
Chicago, IL 60607
Tel: 312-782-8424
Email: info@ift.org
http://www.ift.org

For consumer fact sheets, games for kids, information on issues in the food science industry, and food safety news, visit the NFPA website or contact
National Food Processors Association (NFPA)
1350 I Street, NW, Suite 300
Washington, DC 20005
Tel: 202-639-5900

Email: nfpa@nfpa-food.org
http://www.nfpa-food.org

For national news on agriculture and food issues, contact
U.S. Department of Agriculture
1400 Independence Avenue, SW
Washington, DC 20250
http://www.usda.gov

For information on food safety, contact
U.S. Food and Drug Administration
5600 Fishers Lane
Rockville, MD 20857
Tel: 888-463-6332
http://www.fda.gov

For information and activities that explore the science behind cooking, visit
The Accidental Scientist: The Science of Cooking
http://www.exploratorium.edu/cooking

Food Writers and Editors

What Food Writers and Editors Do

Food writers and editors deal with the written word, whether the completed work is the printed page, broadcast, or computer screen. They tend to write about or edit all things related to food and beverages, such as recipes, new food products, meal planning and preparation, grocery shopping, cooking utensils and related products, and establishments that serve food and beverages.

Food writers need to be able to write very descriptively, since the reader will not be able to taste, touch, or smell the product they are writing about. Food writers use their skills to write about many different things. They might write a press release about a new food product to be distributed to food editors at numerous newspapers and magazines. They may write a story about seasonal fruits and vegetables for a local television news broadcast. They may write an article for a women's magazine about new cooking utensils that make meal preparation easier for amateur chefs. They may write a review about the new restaurant that just opened.

Perhaps the most infamous type of food writer is the *food/restaurant critic*. The critic needs to be objective and fair

To Become a Successful Food Writer and Editor, You Should . . .

- ○ have a love of food and everything to do with food
- ○ be creative
- ○ be curious and willing to try new types of food
- ○ be able to express your opinions and ideas clearly
- ○ have the ability to work under tight deadlines

EXPLORING

○ Take cooking classes, attend ethnic festivals and food events, and tour different food-related businesses.

○ Experiment with different types of restaurants and cuisines. After dining at a new restaurant, write about the experience. Review your writing. It is objective? Descriptive? Informative? Edit and rewrite it until you are satisfied with it.

○ Explore writing and editing by working as a reporter or writer on school newspapers, yearbooks, and literary magazines. If you cannot work for the school paper, try to land a part-time job on a local newspaper or newsletter.

with any type of product or restaurant review. When dining at a restaurant, he or she also needs to remain anonymous, which is not always easy.

Food editors polish the work of a food writer into a finished article or book. They correct grammar, spelling, and style, and check all the facts, especially where recipes are concerned. They make sure that the writing adheres to style guidelines and is appropriate for the intended audience. When working for a magazine or newspaper, food editors may also plan the editorial content of an entire food section. This section may range in size from as little as half of a page to a multiple-page spread. Their duties may include assigning stories to staff or freelance writers, as well as assigning photography or artwork assignments as needed, to accompany the articles and recipes.

Education and Training

Most food writing and editing jobs require a college education. Some employers desire communications or journalism training in college. Others require culinary coursework. Most schools offer courses in journalism and some have more specialized courses in book publishing, publication management, and newspaper and magazine writing.

Earnings

The International Association of Culinary Professionals (IACP) compiled a list of median salaries in 2002 for careers in the

On the Web

Check out the websites of some of the following popular food magazines:

Bon Appetit
http://www.epicurious.com/bonappetit

Cook's Illustrated
http://www.cooksillustrated.com

Cuisine
http://www.cuisinemagazine.com

Fine Cooking
http://www.taunton.com/finecooking

Gourmet
http://www.epicurious.com/gourmet

culinary field, including the following: cookbook author, $5,000 to $10,000 for their first book; cookbook editor, $27,000 to $85,000 annually; magazine food editor, $41,000 to $80,000 annually; newspaper food editor, $39,000 to $61,000 annually; food writer on staff at a publication, $19,000 to $40,000 annually; and freelance food writer, $100 to $1,000 per story.

In addition to their salaries, many food writers and editors receive additional compensation. Most food critics, for example, have the meals they eat at a restaurant for the purpose of a review paid for by their employer. Some food writers and editors also receive travel expenses to cover expenditures such as mileage from driving to cover local events, or airfare and hotel accommodations for covering out-of-town industry events.

Outlook

The employment of food writers and editors is expected to increase about as fast as the average rate over the next several years. Individuals entering this field should realize that the competition for jobs is intense.

FOR MORE INFO

This organization provides a wealth of industry information at its website.
International Association of Culinary Professionals
304 West Liberty Street, Suite 201
Louisville, KY 40202
Tel: 502-581-9786
Email: iacp@hqtrs.com
http://www.iacp.com

This organization offers an online newsletter and magazine at its website.
International Food, Wine & Travel Writers Association
PO Box 8249
Calabasas, CA 91372
Tel: 818-999-9959
http://www.ifwtwa.org

The following organization's website provides information on issues facing food writers and editors, such as ethics, spelling guidelines, and criticism guidelines.
Association of Food Journalists
http://www.afjonline.com

This website offers online courses and a newsletter on writing about food.
Food Writing
Email: editor@food-writing.com
http://www.food-writing.com

Grain Merchants

What Grain Merchants Do

Grain merchants take the grain grown by farmers and deliver it to the public. People need grain year-round, but farmers can harvest only when the grain is ripe. Thus, grain merchants buy, store, inspect, process, and transport the raw grain. This ensures that there is always enough to meet the public's needs, regardless of shortages and surpluses.

Grain merchants may work independently if they have enough money, but many merchants work for grain corporations or farmer-owned cooperatives. In either case, there are two major specialists who perform different functions in this occupation: *grain buyers* and *grain managers*.

Grain buyers evaluate and buy grain for resale and milling. They select the type of grains to order based on current demand and predictions of needs in the future. They arrange for the transportation and storage of the grain and also identify possible resale markets. Grain buyers may buy and store grain directly from the farmer, or they may work in a large terminal elevator in such grain centers as Chicago, Minneapolis, or Kansas City. (Grain is often stored in and dispensed from large buildings called grain elevators or terminal elevators.)

Terminal-elevator buyers get their grain from county elevators rather than directly from the farmer. Other buyers work for food processors, selecting the right type of grain for their products.

Popular Types of Grain

- barley
- corn
- millet
- oats
- rice
- rye
- sorghum
- wheat

EXPLORING

○ If you live in a grain-growing area, take a tour of a county or terminal elevator.

○ If you live in a city, take a tour of a commodities exchange or meet with a grain broker.

○ Joining the Future Farmers of America will teach you about current agricultural issues.

Grain managers work at terminal elevators or other holding facilities. They inspect all the grain that comes to the holding terminal and calculate its market value. They may also send samples to federal grain inspection agencies for analysis. As managers of local or county grain elevators, they keep daily records on the kinds and grades of grain received, prices paid, amounts purchased, and the amount in storage. They also supervise grain elevator workers.

Many grain merchants travel in the course of their work, and as they learn about different kinds of markets and firms, they may change jobs several times. Those working in this field must learn all they can about the grain market. This includes knowledge of weather, crop size and quality, transportation and storage costs, government regulations and policies, and supply and demand—whatever might affect grain and grain prices.

Education and Training

In high school, take classes in agriculture, business, mathematics, and science. Although you may be able to get some assistant positions with only a high school diploma, many grain merchants have undergraduate or graduate degrees in agriculture, economics, or business management from a college or university. However, two-year programs are also available and can open many doors for you.

Many students get summer jobs at grain elevators while they are still in school. They are hired for full-time positions when they graduate. Others may begin work as clerks or runners in a brokerage or grain merchant firm and then work their way up to becoming a broker or buyer. Still others work for state and federal government agencies, where their responsibilities include making inspections, seeing that regulations are met, and granting warehouse and broker licenses.

Grain merchants in commodity futures, who deal directly with the public, must be licensed by the federal government.

Earnings

As with other brokers, some grain merchants work on a commission basis and others work for a straight salary. Earnings vary depending on the size of the employer, the experience of the employee, and the specific job responsibilities. Beginning grain merchants can expect to earn between $18,000 and $26,000 a year. Experienced grain merchants earn between $42,000 and $74,000 annually.

Outlook

The employment of purchasing agents and buyers of farm products is expected to increase about as fast as the average for all occupations over the next several years. It is often difficult to predict how successful this industry will be each year

To Be a Successful Grain Merchant, You Should . . .

- have an excellent rapport with farmers and other suppliers—this will help you get a good price on the grain, favorable payment terms, quick delivery on emergency orders, or help in obtaining the grain during times of scarcity
- have good communication skills
- work well under pressure
- be persuasive, diplomatic, and cooperative
- have good judgment and be dependable and trustworthy

FOR MORE INFO

To learn about current issues affecting grain companies and their employees, contact
Grain Elevator and Processing Society
301 4th Avenue South, Suite 365
PO Box 15026
Minneapolis, MN 55415-0026
Tel: 612-339-4625
Email: info@geaps.com
http://www.geaps.com

For information about agricultural education and careers, contact
National Future Farmers of America Organization
National FFA Center
PO Box 68960
6060 FFA Drive
Indianapolis, IN 46268-0960
Tel: 317-802-6060
http://www.ffa.org

For history and fun facts about grain, visit the following websites:
The Maize Page
http://maize.agron.iastate.edu

RiceWeb
http://www.riceweb.org

because changes in the weather, economy, and government affect growth in this field.

The populations of small agricultural communities are decreasing rapidly in some parts of the country, particularly in the Plains states. However, even though many of the grain elevators are closing in these areas as farmers look for more stable sources of income, grain is still in great demand around the world. Agribusiness professionals, consultants, and the U.S. government are all involved in increasing this demand by searching for new, efficient uses for grain. Scientific advances will also aid in the storage and processing of grain.

Meat Packing Workers

What Meat Packing Workers Do

Meat packing workers kill cattle, hogs, sheep, and poultry using methods that do not cause pain to the animals. They cut, process, and package the meat and other animal parts. They also prepare meat by-products such as shortening, wool, soap, and fertilizers.

There are many different jobs within the meat packing industry. Workers who slaughter and clean the various kinds of animals include *stunners, shacklers, shavers, skinners, poultry dressers,* and *hide trimmers. Offal separators* are workers who separate the parts of the animal that can be eaten from the parts that cannot. Some animal parts are sold to drug companies and are made into medicines.

Casing cleaners and *casing splitters* prepare intestines to be made into sausage casings, surgical thread, or violin strings. *Butchers* use knives, cleavers, and saws to cut the meat into portions. *Meat boners* and *poultry boners* remove bones before the meat is packaged. Meat that will not be sold fresh must be preserved. Some of the workers who preserve meats are *picklers, dry curers, smoked-meat preparers,* and *smokers.* Making sausage, bologna, and wieners requires several types of skilled workers. These include *sausage-meat trimmers, meat grinders, seasoning*

Did You Know?

- Approximately 440,000 workers are employed in the animal production industry.
- The meat and poultry industry is the largest branch of U.S. agriculture, with sales of more than $100 billion in 2000.
- Ninety-five percent of Americans consume some type of meat each year.
- The average American consumed 218.6 pounds of meat and poultry in 2002.

Source: U.S. Department of Labor, American Meat Institute

EXPLORING

○ Talk to workers at a local meat packing plant about their work.

○ High school students may start out in apprenticeships, learning to cut meat and perform other semi-skilled tasks.

○ Summer or part-time jobs in meat packing plants can provide valuable experience for beginners in the field.

mixers, stuffers, and *linkers.* Other meat packing workers include *turkey-roll makers, pork-cutlet makers,* and *ham-rolling-machine operators.*

Meat packing workers also process by-products of animals, such as lard and animal feed. *Lard bleachers* and *refiners* cook and filter animal fat. *Hasher operators* and *rendering-equipment tenders* process waste, such as tendons and cartilage, from the slaughtering operation.

Meat packing workers work in a wide variety of settings, from wholesalers and distributors to huge plants or even multinational corporations. Slaughterhouses, meatpacking plants, and other places employing meat packing workers are located throughout the United States.

Meat packing work can be unpleasant and sometimes dangerous. Workers wear protective clothing to guard against slipping and falling or cutting or burning themselves. Good eyesight, color vision, depth perception, and manual skill are important for avoiding injuries in meat packing industry jobs. Workers who are strong, careful, hard-working, and dependable can move up to become supervisors or managers.

Education and Training

To prepare for a career in this field, take high school courses in agriculture, biology, and technical/shop. Chemistry, health, and family and consumer science courses will also be helpful.

Most meat packing workers learn their skills on the job rather than in a formal educational or classroom setting. Usually employers hire high school graduates for jobs in the meat packing industry, but some jobs have no educational requirements. Workers who want to advance or find better jobs may want to investigate training courses at colleges and universities. A list of schools is available from the American Association of Meat Processors (http://www.aamp.com).

Growing concern about the safety of meats has led employers to offer extensive training in food safety to employees. All meat processing workers follow the guidelines established by Hazard Analysis and Critical Control Points, a food-safety production system designed to prevent food-safety problems.

Earnings

Meat packing workers earn annual salaries of approximately $20,000. Salaries range from $11,000 a year to more than $30,000 a year. Workers with more skills and experience earn higher salaries. Meat packing workers who are members of a union generally receive good fringe benefits, including paid vacations, sick leave, pension plans, paid holidays, and life and health insurance. Benefits can vary greatly for nonunion workers.

More than a Food Source

In addition to providing people with a good source of nutrition, animal by-products are used to create a wide variety of useful goods, including

- leather
- surgical sutures
- violin strings
- tires
- soap
- brushes
- buttons
- cosmetics
- glue
- fertilizer
- floor wax
- matches
- crayons
- chalk
- rubber

Source: Animal Industry Foundation

FOR MORE INFO

For information about food safety and educational opportunities for meat packing workers, contact
American Association of Meat Processors
PO Box 269
Elizabethtown, PA 17022
Tel: 717-367-1168
Email: info@aamp.com
http://www.aamp.com

For industry statistics, contact
American Meat Institute
1150 Connecticut Avenue, NW,
12th Floor
Washington, DC 20036
Tel: 202-587-4200
http://www.meatami.org

Outlook

The growing automation of many meat packing and processing activities is expected to reduce the need for production workers. Workers displaced by machines are usually moved to other jobs in the plant, so entering the industry as an unskilled worker has become more difficult. Because turnover among these workers is fairly high, however, jobs are available for some entry-level workers. As these workers become more skilled, it may be easier for them to find work at different plants. The increased competition for positions, however, has clearly given an edge to high school graduates.

Employment growth of lower skilled meat, poultry, and fish cutters—who work primarily in meat packing, poultry, and fish processing plants—is expected to increase about as fast as the average for all occupations.

Restaurant and Food Service Managers

What Restaurant and Food Service Managers Do

Restaurant and food service managers are responsible for the overall operation of restaurants and other establishments that serve food. Managers usually hire and train their employees. Restaurant and food service managers are responsible for buying the food and equipment necessary for the operation of the restaurant or facility, and they may help with menu planning. They inspect the premises periodically to ensure compliance with health and sanitation regulations. Restaurant and food service managers perform many clerical and financial duties, such as keeping records, directing payroll operations, handling large sums of money, and taking inventories. Managers also usually supervise advertising and special sales programs.

The work of restaurant and food service managers usually involves daily contact with customers. Managers take suggestions, handle complaints, and

Did You Know?

○ There are approximately 386,000 restaurant and food service managers in the United States.

○ More than 800 community and junior colleges, technical institutes, or other institutions offer training programs in restaurant and food service management.

○ More than 150 colleges and universities offer four-year programs leading to a bachelor's degree in restaurant and management or institutional food service management.

○ Restaurant and food service managers typically work more than 50 hours a week.

Source: U.S. Department of Labor

EXPLORING

○ You can learn about food preparation and food service by getting involved in planning and budgeting for family, religious, or community events that involve food. Try to participate in every aspect of such events, including cooking, assigning tasks to others, buying ingredients and supplies, organizing dining areas, and hosting.

○ Visit a restaurant and observe the many different types of workers—including the manager—that it takes to keep things operating efficiently.

○ Ask your teacher or parent to set up a presentation by a restaurant or food service manager. Be prepared with questions such as: How did you train for this field?, What are the pros and cons of your job?, What advice would you give to someone who is interested in this field?

try to create a friendly atmosphere in which diners can enjoy themselves.

Very large restaurants may employ *assistant managers,* an *executive chef, food and beverage managers,* and a *wine steward* in addition to restaurant and food service managers. These workers are trained to supervise the kitchen staff. They also are responsible for all food and drink preparation in the restaurant.

In some cases, the manager of a restaurant is also its owner. The *owner-manager* of a restaurant is likely to be involved in service functions, sometimes operating the cash register, waiting on tables, and performing a wide variety of tasks. *Nonowner-managers* of large restaurants or institutional food service facilities are usually employees who are paid a salary. They may work in dining rooms and cafeterias of hotels, department stores, factories, schools, hospitals, ships, trains, and private clubs.

Education and Training

Restaurant and food service managers need to have experience in all areas of restaurant and food service work before they can advance to the level of manager. They must be familiar with food preparation, food service, sanitary rules, and financial operations. Managers also must have good business skills in order to manage a budget and a staff. They apply this business knowledge as they buy machinery, equipment, and food.

Some colleges offer programs in restaurant management. These programs combine classroom work with on-the-job experience. Some graduates of technical or vocational schools can quickly qualify for management training.

Some managers learn their skills through a special apprenticeship program sponsored by the National Restaurant Association. Many restaurant and food service managers start as waiters or kitchen staff, and as they gain on-the-job experience, they take on more responsibility and eventually move into management positions.

The National Restaurant Association Educational Foundation and the International Food Service Executives Association offer voluntary certification to restaurant and food service managers.

Earnings

Salaries of restaurant and food service managers vary depending on size of the facility, location, and amount of business. Food service managers earned median salaries of $37,260 in 2003, according to the U.S. Department of Labor. Salaries ranged from less than $22,900 to $66,970 or more annually. In

Earnings by Industry

Type of Career	Mean Annual Earnings
Support Activities for Air Transportation	$68,990
Traveler Accommodation	$45,910
Full-Service Restaurants	$42,420
Limited-Service Eating Places	$40,460
Elementary and Secondary Schools	$39,420

Source: U.S. Department of Labor, 2003

FOR MORE INFO

For information on accredited education programs, contact
International Council on Hotel, Restaurant, and Institutional Education
2613 North Parham Road, 2nd Floor
Richmond, VA 23294
Tel: 804-346-4800
Email: info@chrie.org
http://chrie.org

For information on education and careers, contact
National Restaurant Association Educational Foundation
175 West Jackson Boulevard, Suite 1500
Chicago, IL 60604-2702
Tel: 800-765-2122
Email: info@nraef.org
http://www.nraef.org

For information on training, contact
International Food Service Executives Association
836 San Bruno Avenue
Henderson, NV 89015
Tel: 888-234-3732
http://www.ifsea.org

general, large restaurants in and around cities pay the highest salaries. Mean annual earnings for managers of full-service restaurants were $42,420 in 2003, according to the U.S. Department of Labor. In addition to a base salary, most managers receive bonuses based on profits, which can range from $2,000 to $7,500 a year.

Outlook

Employment for restaurant and food service managers will grow about as fast as the average over the next several years. Many job openings will arise from the need to replace managers retiring from the workforce. Also, population growth will result in an increased demand for eating establishments. Managers who have earned bachelor's or associate's degrees in restaurant management or related areas will have the best employment prospects.

Supermarket Managers

What Supermarket Managers Do

Supermarket managers help run the daily operations of grocery stores. Managers include store managers, assistant store managers, courtesy booth/service desk managers, customer service managers, receiving managers, and managers of such departments as bakery, deli/food service, food court, front end, grocery, meat/seafood, produce, frozen foods, pharmacy, and produce/floral. The size and location of the store determines how many of these management levels exist in each store. In a small, family-owned grocery, the manager and owner may be the same person.

Supermarket managers work with employees and customers all day. They are in charge of the business aspects of the store, including budgets, scheduling, and inventory. Each store may employ 250 or more people, so skill in interviewing, hiring, and managing workers is very important.

Supermarket managers supervise many types of workers, including cashiers, clerks, baggers, stock personnel, butchers, bakers, deli workers, janitors and cleaners, human resource professionals, accounting professionals, security workers, advertising and marketing workers, information technology

Largest Supermarket and Grocery Sales (by 2003 grocery sales)

1. Wal-Mart Supercenters
2. The Kroger Company
3. Albertson's
4. Safeway
5. Ahold USA
6. Costco Wholesale Group
7. Sam's Club
8. Publix Super Markets
9. Delhaize America
10. Winn-Dixie Stores

Source: *Directory of Supermarket, Grocery & Convenience Store Chains*

EXPLORING

○ Go to a local grocery store on a busy day and a slow day. Study what activities are taking place and how management's role changes from day to day. Get a feel for the pace of a retail environment as a workplace.

○ If you are interested in becoming a supermarket manager, get a job at a supermarket. Any job, from bagger to cashier, will help you understand the industry better. Openings for students are usually available, and it's a great way to find out about the industry.

○ Interview supermarket managers to discuss the things they like and do not like about their jobs.

professionals, public relations professionals, and pharmacists and pharmacy technicians (at larger chain supermarkets that have a pharmacy).

Planning is an important part of the supermarket manager's job. Supermarket managers plan promotions and budgets while also setting up holiday promotions and displays. Because some grocery stores are open 24 hours a day, managers may work different schedules each week. They often work late hours, weekends, and holidays.

Education and Training

In high school, you should take English, business, speech, computer science, and math classes to help you prepare for supermarket work. Classes in marketing, advertising, or statistics will also be helpful.

Supermarket managers need at least a high school diploma to work in this field. While a college degree is not always necessary, there is a trend toward hiring new managers straight out of college. Many people work through the ranks of a grocery store to become a manager, but a new trend it to hire managers with college degrees in business or retail management. Even an associate's degree in retail or business management will give you an advantage over other applicants who have only a high school diploma.

Earnings

According to the U.S. Department of Labor, grocery store managers earned median annual salaries of $32,320 in 2003. First-

A supermarket manager and a worker examine a package of meat in a supermarket. (Ken Hammond, USDA)

line supervisors/managers of retail workers earned salaries that ranged from less than $18,920 to $56,540 or more in 2003. In general, starting managers can expect to make $30,000 a year. Department managers at large stores average $50,000 annually.

Did You Know?

○ The first supermarket, King Kullen Grocery Company, opened in New York in 1930.

○ Saturday is the most popular day for grocery shopping. The next most popular days are Sunday and Friday.

○ There are 33,841 supermarkets (grocery stores that generate $2 million or more in annual sales) in the United States.

○ The average consumer makes two trips to the supermarket each week.

○ The average family spends $90 each week on groceries.

Source: Food Marketing Institute

FOR MORE INFO

For industry-related statistics, contact
Food Marketing Institute
655 15th Street, NW
Washington, DC 20005
Tel: 202-452-8444
Email: fmi@fmi.org
http://www.fmi.org

District managers earn average salaries of $100,000 annually. These salary numbers may include bonuses that are standard in the industry. Pay is affected by management level, the size of the store, and the location.

Benefits are also good, with most major employers offering health insurance, vacation pay, and sick pay. While some supermarket workers are covered by a union, managers are not required to pay union dues and do not receive overtime pay.

Outlook

Managers in the supermarket industry should expect growth that is slower than the average over the next several years. While the number of stores (and managers needed to run them) is decreasing, the need for managers with specialized skills (in managing specific departments, for example) and ample experience will continue.

Winemakers

What Winemakers Do

Winemakers, sometimes called *enologists*, are involved in all phases of wine production and must have a thorough understanding of the business. As an expert in viticulture (the growing of grapes), the enologist has many important decisions to make. Perhaps the most important decision is which grapes to grow. Winemakers study the different European and American grapes and then decide which varieties are best for the soil and climate of their land. Different varieties of grapes have different planting, pruning, and harvesting times.

Winemakers must keep up-to-date on all of the new technology that comes along to help the winemaking process. For example, winemakers might have to decide whether to use highly mechanical grape harvesters and crushers, which speed up the entire winemaking process but might affect the quality. The winemaker also has to consult with staff members about the testing and crushing of the grapes and their cooling, filtering, and bottling.

As the business managers of a winery, winemakers must be organized and knowledgeable in financial matters. For example, they must have the ability to analyze profit-and-loss statements and other parts of balance

Who Drinks the Most Wine?

1. France
2. Italy
3. United States
4. Germany
5. Spain
6. Argentina
7. China
8. United Kingdom
9. Russia
10. Romania

Source: U.S. Department of Commerce, 2001

A winemaker checks a sample of aging white wine from an oak cask in the winery's warehouse. (Charles O'Rear/Corbis)

sheets. Winemakers are also involved with the marketing of the wines, including making such crucial decisions as where the wines will be sold and at what price. They usually oversee all matters involving their staffs, including hiring, firing, and setting salaries.

EXPLORING

○ Visit websites and read books and magazines (such as *American Wine Society Journal*) about winemaking.
○ Take a tour of a winery and watch winemakers in action.
○ Ask your teacher or parent to arrange an information interview with someone who works in a winery.

Education and Training

Winemaking is an increasingly competitive field, and you will likely need a college degree to obtain an entry-level job. In college, you should major in viticulture or horticulture. Some wineries offer on-the-job training in the form of apprenticeship for high school graduates. However, most entry-level positions go to college graduates, so a college degree is recommended.

Wineries of any size must be licensed both by the state in which

To Be a Successful Winemaker, You Should . . .

- have excellent verbal and written communication skills
- be able to handle multiple tasks and priorities
- be able to take direction from supervisors and work well on a team
- have basic computer knowledge
- have a familiarity with the Bureau of Alcohol, Tobacco, Firearms, and Explosives and state regulations concerning winemaking, handling, and transport
- have the physical strength to climb stairs, work on high platforms, lift and carry 40 pounds, bend, squat, and stretch
- be at least 21 years of age

they are located and the Bureau of Alcohol, Tobacco, Firearms, and Explosives. Owners of wineries are responsible for obtaining and maintaining these licenses. Winemakers must be at least 21 years of age.

Earnings

Beginning salary levels for winemakers depend on the applicant's education level and the size of the winery. The average beginning salary is $25,000 per year. Experienced winemakers

On the Web

History of Wine
http://www.history-of-wine.com

Wine Associations and Related Organizations
http://www.wineinstitute.org/communications/resource_lists/associations_resource.htm

WineLoversPage
http://wineloverspage.com

FOR MORE INFO

For industry information, contact
American Society for Enology and Viticulture
PO Box 1855
Davis, CA 95617-1855
Tel: 530-753-3142
Email: society@asev.org
http://www.asev.org

For information on education and chapter events, including competitions and wine tastings, contact
American Wine Society
PO Box 3330
Durham, NC 27702
Tel: 919-403-0022
http://www.americanwinesociety.com

earn between $50,000 and $85,000 per year. Top winemakers and other executives at some larger wineries may earn more than $200,000 a year.

Outlook

Job growth is tied to the size and quality of grape harvests, the success of wine production, and the demand for American wines in the United States and in other countries. Technological advances in wine production may create more job opportunities.

Job opportunities will be best in California, where most of the U.S. wineries are located. Most California wine is cultivated in the San Joaquin, Napa, and Sonoma valleys, the central coast, and the Sierra foothills.

Glossary

accredited   approved as meeting established standards for providing good training and education; this approval is usually given to a school or a program in a school by an independent organization of professionals

apprentice   person who is learning a trade by working under the supervision of a skilled worker; apprentices often receive classroom instruction in addition to their supervised practical experience

associate's degree   academic rank or title granted by a community or junior college or similar institution to graduates of a two-year program of education beyond high school

bachelor's degree   academic rank or title given to a person who has completed a four-year program of study at a college or university; also called an undergraduate degree or baccalaureate

career   occupation for which a worker receives training and has an opportunity for advancement

certified   approved as meeting established requirements for skill, knowledge, and experience in a particular field; people are certified by the organization of professionals in their field

college   higher education institution that is above the high school level

community college   public two-year college attended by students who do not usually live at the college; a graduate of a community college receives an associate's degree and may transfer to a four-year college or university to complete a bachelor's degree

diploma   certificate or document given by a school to show that a person has completed a course or has graduated from the school

distance education   type of educational program that allows students to take classes and complete their education by mail or the Internet

doctorate   highest academic rank or title granted by a graduate school to a person who has completed a two- to three-year program after having received a master's degree

fringe benefit   payment or benefit to an employee in addition to regular wages or salary; examples of fringe benefits include a pension, a paid vacation, and health or life insurance

graduate school   school that people may attend after they have received their bachelor's degree; people who complete an educational program at a graduate school earn a master's degree or a doctorate

intern   advanced student (usually one with at least some college training) who is employed in a job that is intended to provide supervised practical career experience

internship   (1) the position or job of an intern; (2) period of time when a person is an intern

junior college   two-year college that offers courses like those in the first half of a four-year college program; graduates of a junior college usually receive an associate's degree and may transfer to a four-year college or university to complete a bachelor's degree

liberal arts   subjects covered by college courses that develop broad general knowledge rather than specific occupational skills; the liberal arts are often considered to include philosophy, literature and the arts, history, language, and some courses in the social sciences and natural sciences

major (in college)   academic field in which a student specializes and receives a degree

master's degree   academic rank or title granted by a graduate school to a person who has completed a one- or two-year program after having received a bachelor's degree

online education   academic study that is performed by using a computer and the Internet

pension   amount of money paid regularly by an employer to a former employee after he or she retires from working

scholarship   gift of money to a student to help the student pay for further education

social studies   courses of study (such as civics, geography, and history) that deal with how human societies work

starting salary   salary paid to a newly hired employee; the starting salary is usually a smaller amount than is paid to a more experienced worker

technical college   private or public college offering two- or four-year programs in technical subjects; technical colleges offer courses in both general and technical subjects and award associate's degrees and bachelor's degrees

undergraduate   student at a college or university who has not yet received a degree

undergraduate degree   see **bachelor's degree**

union   organization whose members are workers in a particular industry or company; the union works to gain better wages, benefits, and working conditions for its members; also called a labor union or trade union

wage   money that is paid in return for work done, especially money paid on the basis of the number of hours or days worked

Index of Job Titles

Browse and Learn More

Books

Cunningham, Marion. *Cooking with Children: 15 Lessons for Children, Age 7 and Up, Who Really Want to Learn to Cook.* New York: Knopf, 1995.

D'Amico, Joan. *The Science Chef: 100 Fun Food Experiments and Recipes for Kids.* Hoboken, N.J.: John Wiley & Sons, 1994.

D'Amico, Joan. *The United States Cookbook: Fabulous Foods and Fascinating Facts From All 50 States.* Hoboken, N.J.: John Wiley & Sons, 2000.

Donovan, Mary. *Careers for Gourmets & Others Who Relish Food.* 2nd ed. New York: McGraw-Hill, 2002.

Eddy, Jackie. *The Absolute Beginner's Cookbook: Or, How Long Do I Cook a 3-Minute Egg?* New York: Gramercy Books, 2003.

Fernandez-Armesto, Felipe. *Near a Thousand Tables: A History of Food.* New York: Free Press, 2002.

Haduch, Bill, and Rich Stromoski. *Food Rules! The Stuff You Munch, Its Crunch, Its Punch, and Why You Sometimes Lose Your Lunch.* New York: Puffin Books, 2001.

Heyhoe, Kate. *Cooking With Kids for Dummies.* New York: For Dummies, 1999.

Maynard, Chris. *Kitchen Science.* New York: DK Publishing Inc., 2001.

Otterbourg, Robert K. *Careers in the Food Services Industry* (Success Without College). Hauppauge, N.Y.: Barron's Educational Series, 1999.

Pasternak, Ceel, and Linda Thornburg. *Cool Careers for Girls in Food.* Manassas Park, Va.: Impact Publications, 1999.

Websites

4-H Clubs
http://www.4h-usa.org

Cookalotamus
http://www.cookalotamus.com

Cyber Space Farm
http://www.cyberspaceag.com

Discover Hershey: Making Chocolate
http://www.hersheys.com/discover/chocolate.asp

Farm Service Agency for Kids
http://www.fsa.usda.gov/fsakids

Food and Drug Administration Kids
http://www.fda.gov/oc/opacom/kids

Food Museum
http://www.foodmuseum.com

National Future Farmers of America
http://www.ffa.org

Nutrition Explorations
http://www.nutritionexplorations.org

PBS: Empty Oceans, Empty Nets
http://www.pbs.org/emptyoceans

Science of Cooking
http://www.exploratorium.edu/cooking

U.S. Department of Agriculture for Kids
http://www.usda.gov/news/usdakids

U.S. Department of Agriculture-National Agricultural Statistics Service Kids
http://www.usda.gov/nass/nasskids/nasskids.htm

Whole Foods Market: Cool Stuff for Kids
http://www.wholefoodsmarket.com/kids

World of Tastes
http://www.topics-mag.com/foods/world-of-food.htm